P9-ELV-299

BRAVE YOUNG REFUGEES

Allan Zullo

SCHOLASTIC INC.

To my wife, Kathy,
who has made 50 trips with me around the sun,
each one a stellar adventure.
—A.Z.

ISBN 978-1-338-08811-3

10 9 8 7 6 5 4 3 2 1   17 18 19 20 21

Printed in the U.S.A.   40
First printing 2017

Book design by Cheung Tai

ACKNOWLEDGMENTS

★

I wish to extend my gratitude to the persons featured in this book for their willingness to relive, in personal interviews with me, their often heart-wrenching and emotional memories of the hardships and horrors they experienced as child refugees.

Special thanks go to the following for their much appreciated cooperation and help in providing me with contact information: Amy Crownover, marketing and communications director, New American Pathways, Atlanta, Georgia; Harriet Kuhr, executive director, International Rescue Committee, Charlottesville, Virginia; Louisa Merchant, coordinator of refugee ministries, All Saints' Episcopal Church, Atlanta; Blake Ortman, community organizer, Jubilee Partners, Comer, Georgia; and Kia Presley, public relations manager, Tara Dowdell Group, New York.

I also want to thank family and friends of the former refugees who spoke with me, including Trien Vo, Ha Vo Green, Olivier Mandevu, Pa Saw Paw, and Etienne Mazimpaka.

AUTHOR'S NOTE

★

You are about to read 10 incredible true stories of what young refugees endured when, through no fault of their own, they were torn from their homes by war or genocide—the deliberate mass killing of a large ethnic group—and had to flee their country. They were unable to return to their homelands because of violence, so their lives were put on hold—in some cases for years—while they held on to the uncertain hope for a better life.

They found that better life. They no longer suffer from the horrors of their childhoods because they are settled in the United States, leading happy, productive lives. They are proof positive of why America is the greatest nation on earth.

Their stories are based exclusively on the personal, lengthy interviews that I conducted with each person. Using real names, dates, and places, I wrote the stories as factual and truthful versions of the refugees' recollections.

If you see an asterisk after a name, it means the person is real but the name is not. That's because the refugee can't remember it, doesn't know it, or wants anonymity for that individual to protect him or her and family members from possible vengeance in their native country.

Some of what you will read in the following pages is disturbing because that's the way it really happened. It's hard to imagine that anyone, especially children, could bear so much suffering. But they persevered. And now they are thriving here in a free society.

The book features stories of young refugees from Syria, Iraq, Burma (also known as Myanmar), Bosnia, Somalia, Liberia, Democratic Republic of Congo, Rwanda, Cambodia, and Vietnam. Among the refugees you will get to know are:

• Nam Vo, a Vietnamese boy who was crammed with his parents, three siblings, and forty other refugees aboard an overcrowded fishing boat in the South China Sea. After days of eluding pirates and navy gunships, their boat was caught in a vicious typhoon. Fearing the worst, his father told the family, "At least we will die together. If we stayed in Vietnam, we would all die another way."

• Judith Ngena, a Congolese teenage girl. When rebels invaded her town, she and her family fled to a refugee camp in nearby Burundi. But the rebels attacked the camp and killed 166 people, including her mother, father, and brother.

• Moustafa Aldouri, a Muslim teenager, who on his way to school was seized in Baghdad, Iraq, by a kidnapping gang, one of hundreds collecting ransom from families and funneling the money to terrorist groups. He was mistreated for nine days while his frantic parents tried to raise the money to free him.

Accepting refugees into our country has been a topic of national debate, especially in Congress. Some people want to close our doors to refugees, such as Muslims from Middle Eastern countries, out of concern that terrorists might be among them. But Muslim refugees who are approved for immigration to the US must pass a thorough screening process that can last two years or longer. Besides, they don't commit acts of terror; they are the *victims* of acts of terror. That's why they are refugees.

Another argument against resettling refugees here is that we should take care of our own first. However, Americans haven't lost everything they own and been uprooted from their homes because of a bloody conflict or tyranny. Refugees have. Besides, what does "our own" mean anyway? Just our family, friends, and neighbors? Just members of our ethnic group or religion or only American-born citizens?

Consider the biblical parable of the Good Samaritan (Luke 10:25-37), which teaches us to love all those in need. Luke doesn't add the condition "as long as they share your nationality, ethnicity, or religion."

Let's also keep in mind the words at the base of the Statue of Liberty, the gleaming symbol of freedom admired the world over: "Give me your tired, your poor/ Your huddled masses yearning to breathe free/ The wretched refuse of your teeming shore." These are not empty words, but a bedrock American principle.

All 10 refugees featured in this book are now American citizens. Of those mentioned in this author's note, Judith, the married mother of four, is a nurse's assistant in New York; Moustafa is a refugee resettlement counselor in New Jersey; and Nam, the married father of three, is a board-certified nephrologist (kidney specialist) in North Carolina.

Oh, there is one more thing you should know: When my wife, Kathy, went into sudden kidney failure in 2012, it was Dr. Nam Vo—the once scrawny, frightened, seasick refugee from Vietnam—who saved her life.

—Allan Zullo

CONTENTS

ESCAPE OF THE BOAT PEOPLE

NAM VO
Vietnam

I n the 1960s and early 1970s, the communist regime of North Vietnam and the Viet Cong fought against South Vietnam and its main ally, the United States. American forces eventually withdrew, and two years later, in 1975, the communists took over total control of both countries, turning them into one—the Republic of Vietnam. The conflict claimed the lives of more than 3 million people, including more than 58,000 American troops.

After the war ended, the victorious communists set out to punish those who fought against them by executing an estimated 65,000 Vietnamese and shipping another million people to "re-education" camps—which were slave-labor camps or prisons— where an estimated 165,000 people were tortured and killed. The oppressive, cruel government made life unbearable for millions of citizens and barred them from leaving the country without permission, which it seldom granted.

As a result, hundreds of thousands of men, women, and children tried to sneak out of Vietnam. In the largest seagoing exodus of its time, they escaped on leaky, overcrowded fishing boats not fit for the treacherous open waters. Rather than suffer under communism, these "boat people," as they were called, gambled their lives for a chance at a better future. They risked storms and shipwrecks; drowning, starvation, and disease; and vicious pirates bent on robbing, abusing, or murdering them or selling them into slavery.

Despite these perils, the boat people sailed into the South China Sea in their pursuit of liberty. Sadly, many never reached the shores of freedom alive. According to the United Nations High Commission for Refugees, an estimated 200,000 boat people perished between 1975 and 1995. However, more than 800,000 survived, most of them immigrating to the land of the free—the United States.

"Our Father, who art in heaven, hallowed be thy name."

Ten-year-old Nam Vo uttered the words of the Our Father (the Catholic version of the Lord's Prayer), trying to keep up with his parents and three younger siblings, who were reciting the rosary. But it wasn't easy for the slender, floppy-haired boy. He was seasick and scared.

"Thy kingdom come, thy will be done . . ."

For hours and hours in the rain-lashing night, an angry sea churned by a merciless typhoon had battered the rickety fishing boat that was taking him and more than 40 other refugees to what they hoped were their new lives. Now he feared it was taking them to their deaths.

". . . on earth as it is in heaven . . ."

Nam's terror only intensified when lightning illuminated the fright etched on the faces of the passengers. As the wind-whipped waves crashed over the side of the vessel, drenching him and all the other souls onboard, his mother, Thu, clutched the string of plastic beads that made up the rosary and continued to lead the family in prayer. Her tense voice tried to rise above the shrieking gale.

"Give us this day our daily bread . . ."

Nam huddled closer to his father, Trien. Another large wave slammed into the banged-up boat, rocking it so far to starboard that passengers screamed in dread that it would capsize. The vessel righted itself, only to be pounded by the next powerful wave.

". . . and forgive us our trespasses, as we forgive those who trespass against us . . ."

Nam didn't know how much more he could take of this terrifying ordeal. He just wanted to be on land, any land, even the tyrannical country that he and his family had just left.

". . . and lead us not into temptation . . ."

He tried not to think about death, about drowning, about never seeing his mother and father and his sisters Ha, nine, and Hien, seven, and brother Long, five. They, too, were saying the words to the Our Father while also lost in their own thoughts of doom.

". . . but deliver us from evil. Amen."

Holding each other tightly, the Vo family continued reciting the rosary. As they began the next prayer—the Hail Mary—another lightning bolt struck nearby, giving Nam a brief glimpse of his parents' expressions. Neither one looked frightened anymore. There was now a steely calm about them, as if accepting their fate, come what may, because it was in the hands of a higher power. And so the Vos continued the rosary, repeating in groups of 10 the Hail Mary, which ends ". . . Holy Mary, Mother of God, pray for us sinners, now and at the hour of our death. Amen."

Nam was hoping the hour of their death was not now.

Two months after the war ended in 1975, Nam was born in the coastal city of Da Nang, in what had been South Vietnam. Compared to many kids who lived in poverty, he enjoyed a childhood that was better than most. Both his parents had jobs that didn't pay much, but just enough. (The average worker made 430 dollars a year.) Nam and his siblings never lacked for food or clothes and lived in a house with extended family members, including his maternal grandparents. Cousins, aunts, and uncles from nearby villages often stayed over for visits.

His parents did all they could to hide from Nam and his siblings the ugly truth about their communist country—that they were all living in a harsh, unjust society, especially for those who, like them, were not communists and never would be.

Trained by Americans, Trien had flown helicopters for the South Vietnamese Air Force in the war. He was seriously wounded in his right hand during a rescue mission in 1972 when his chopper came under heavy enemy fire. Despite losing one and a half fingers, he managed to pilot his crippled aircraft back to the base. Unable to fly anymore because of his injury, Trien received an honorable discharge.

After losing the war, most who fought in the South Vietnamese military were rounded up and shipped to hard-labor camps, where they toiled for months and even years. Many of Trien's friends died there. Trien was lucky. Although the government accused him of spying and sent him to a "re-education" camp, he was released a month later.

Like so many other anti-communists, Trien wasn't allowed to land a good-paying job even though he was well educated. To make a modest living, he worked with his brother as a carpenter while Thu operated a small tailor shop at the front of their house.

The Vos were hassled often by the police and authorities. Trien had to report to officials every day and seek permission if he wanted to visit relatives outside the city. Repeatedly, Nam saw communists barge into his home unannounced and harass his parents, often demanding money—what they termed "taxes"—from the couple. Not paying up meant imprisonment or other forms of punishment. It was common practice for officials to steal whatever they wanted as payment for these so-called taxes. To protect the family's valuables and gold from being taken, Trien carved a secret hiding place for them in a bedpost.

But the pressure to pay local authorities intensified, forcing Thu to close her shop and secretly work in the home of her neighbor, Tho Le. Fortunately for the Vos, Thu had such a strong following and good reputation that she was able to continue making a living.

When Nam attended elementary school, he began noticing neighbors were abruptly leaving their homes and not returning. He heard rumors that they were escaping Vietnam. He really couldn't understand why. After all, it was a good thing that the two Vietnams were united as one under communism—at least that's what he was taught in class.

He didn't understand that students were being brainwashed to idolize Ho Chi Minh, the country's late communist revolutionary leader who was "the godfather of everything." Portraits, posters, and images of "Uncle Ho," as he was known to children, were everywhere—in classrooms, on the sides of buildings and fences, and on billboards. A public address system would wake up the neighborhood, and children would run out of their houses to exercise and sing songs in honor of Uncle Ho.

Nam and his sister Ha wanted to be good communists in school. If you were an exceptional student who followed the rules and recited the teachings of Uncle Ho, as Nam and Ha did, teachers praised you and gave you a prized red scarf. Nam and Ha were proud to wear their well-earned red scarves.

After Nam came home from school one day, he told his mother about what he learned in history class: "Brave Vietnamese communists fought the Americans and killed the bad people who supported the South Vietnamese government."

"Well, your father was one of those who fought against the communists," Thu replied. "He risked his life to fight for freedom. Is he a bad person?"

"Of course not," Nam replied. "He's a great man."

Little more was spoken about the subject because if authorities knew Trien and Thu were teaching their children about the evils of communism, the Vo kids might never see their parents again.

Although much of Vietnam was Buddhist, the Vos were devout Catholics who attended Mass and prayed as a family every evening. When Nam wasn't in school, he played soccer and learned the guitar. Because his parents were big believers in education, they paid tutors to help improve the kids' skills in math and English.

However, Trien and Thu believed that no matter how bright the children were, the kids' future was dim. Communist authorities were unwilling to consider higher education for the offspring of those, like Trien, who had fought against Ho Chi Minh's forces.

"How are our children going to survive in this country?" Trien said to Thu. "The school teaches Nam and Ha terrible things that aren't true. And the communists are against religion. As strong Catholics, we can't raise our children this way."

"We can't stay here any longer," Thu said.

"Yes, we must escape. It will be dangerous, but it's worth the gamble to give them a shot at a better life."

"We have to keep our plans from the children," Thu said.

"I agree. We can't let anyone know until the last minute. If the government finds out what we're planning, we'll be thrown in jail—or worse."

Although many escape attempts by others had ended in tragedy, Trien and Thu were heartened by reports that tens of thousands of freedom-seeking Vietnamese had successfully fled the country. The adult children of the woman across the street from the Vos had made it to the United States. They were sending her money and packages of clothes and gifts, even a color TV. Nam was envious of her—and began to think, *Just how bad can America be?*

One afternoon in March 1986, two months shy of his 11th birthday, Nam walked home from school and helped his grandfather saw wood. The boy soon sensed something odd was going on. His aunts and uncles—including several from out of town—had gathered and were hugging his parents and crying. The tutored lessons he and Ha were supposed to have had been canceled. *Why is Grandma preparing a special dinner for all of us?* Nam wondered.

Later that evening, Trien and Thu announced to the children, "There's a festival at the beach, and they're showing an outdoor movie. We're all going to see it." Even though it was warm outside, Thu insisted that the barefoot kids wear jackets. Trien, with the two boys on his bicycle, and Thu, with the two girls on hers, rode about 10 miles (16 kilometers) to a beach crowded with festival goers. Both parents also carried bags of what Nam assumed contained treats.

The family milled around until Hy Nguyen, a young man learning to become a priest at the local seminary, showed up. Nam recognized Hy. The seminarian had tried to escape from Vietnam eight times, but each attempt had ended in his capture and a brief jail sentence.

Weeks earlier, Nam had accompanied his mother to church for a meeting with Hy, which the family priest had arranged. While Nam played in the basement, Thu told Hy, "I heard you are planning another escape. Please, you must take my family and me. We are constantly harassed. We can't live like this anymore."

Hy agreed to help the Vo family escape. Thu was thrilled—until she heard it would cost 6,000 dollars. "Yes, it's a lot," Hy explained. "The head organizer and I need the money to secure a boat, hire a captain, buy fuel and supplies, and bribe the police."

Thu and Trien had only about 3,000 dollars in gold bars. However, Thu's friend Tho Le agreed to give them a loan—but only if Thu could convince Hy to take Tho Le and her small twins with the Vos. Hy refused at first. "There would be six children in your group of nine," he explained. "That's too many. If one of them cries, it will blow the entire operation. Besides, there isn't enough room on the boat because many others are escaping with us." However, days later, a few people backed out, so Tho Le and her children were allowed to go. She then paid organizers the fee for her family and the Vos. Hy reminded the parents not to breathe a word of the escape attempt to their kids, claiming, "It's hard for a child to keep a secret."

Now, at the lively beachside festival, Nam was wondering why his parents were acting so jittery. He overheard Hy tell them, "Many people are coming and going, so this is a good time. No one will be suspicious."

A good time for what? Nam wondered. *Suspicious about what?*

Later that night, Hy led the family away from the thinning crowd and toward dunes topped by prickly bushes. Nam's mind was beginning to whirl: the relatives' unexpected visit, the shedding of tears, the special meal, the jackets on a warm night, Hy's appearance. It was all starting to make sense, and that petrified Nam. Suddenly, he felt his whole body tremble.

"You do know what's happening, right?" Thu asked Nam.

He nodded, unable to hide the fear that was enveloping him. "We're escaping."

When Ha realized the family was attempting to flee the

country, she blurted, "But I can't go. I have exams tomorrow." Then she burst into tears.

"Shush," Trien ordered. "We have to be quiet. If you make too much noise, you'll attract the soldiers. And if they discover what we're doing, they'll put me in prison."

Hearing that worry only made Nam and Ha more frightened. Ha continued to cry, causing Nam to repeatedly whisper to her, "Be quiet or we'll all be in trouble." Their younger siblings, Hien and Long, remained silent.

"Split up into smaller groups, hide in the bushes somewhere, and wait for a signal," Hy instructed the Vos. "When you see a flashing light from a fishing boat anchored offshore, go down to the water."

Nam went with his mother, Long took his father's hand, and the girls followed Hy. As Nam and Thu were heading for the brush, a police officer appeared and blocked their way. He pulled out his gun and aimed it at them. Nam was so rattled he could barely breathe. *We've been caught! They'll throw us in jail!* The boy wanted to run but his legs wouldn't move.

"What are you doing here?" the police officer demanded.

"We're waiting for a boat," Thu replied. "Hy Nguyen sent us over here. You do know him, right?" It was her way of asking if Hy had bribed him.

The police officer nodded and holstered his weapon. He pointed to another area farther down the beach and said, "You'll find better cover over there."

Shortly after Nam and his mother hid in the brush, the boy saw officers confront a small group of escapees on the beach. Either because they chickened out or encountered the wrong cops who hadn't been bribed, the people panicked. They took off their jewelry, handed it to the officers, and ran off.

Meanwhile, near another part of the beach, Hy had escorted Ha and Hien to a cemetery and told them to hide behind the tombstones. Ha couldn't stifle her sobs, moaning, "I want to go home." Hien squeezed Ha's hand and said, "Quiet. Do you want us to get caught?"

For hours, the Vos and other escapees waited for the signal. Nam's mind was a jumbled mess of emotions: Fear of the unknown. Excitement about a new adventure. Heartache over leaving loved ones, especially his maternal grandparents. "I never got the chance to say good-bye to Grandma and Grandpa," he whispered to his mother.

"I told Grandma," Thu said. "But I couldn't tell Grandpa. He's such an emotional man that he would have gone crazy with grief and made it difficult for all of us. It's better this way."

"I'm going to miss them," Nam said.

"Yes, I am, too. But sometimes it's necessary to make sacrifices. This is one of those times. Just remember that as hard as it is for them not to see us anymore, they want us to have a chance at freedom and a future."

"Mom, I'm scared."

Thu hugged him and said, "I am, too. We all are."

Midnight passed, and so did 1:00 a.m., with no sign of the boat. Finally, around 2:00 a.m., a light flashed in the distance offshore. "That's our signal," Thu whispered. "That's our boat. Let's go!"

During the dash toward the water, about 100 yards away, Nam yelped in pain. Loose cactus spines in the sand had punctured his bare feet. But there was no time to yank them out. He hobbled to the shoreline, where other escapees, including the rest of his family, were gathering. Minutes later, two men paddled to the beach in a typical Vietnamese basket boat. Made of woven bamboo, the perfectly round craft was about eight feet in diameter and held six to eight people.

With hardly a word spoken, Trien put his wife and children in the basket boat before jumping in. *This is really happening!* Nam thought. He was feeling a rush of elation, which masked his fear of the water from not knowing how to swim. The men paddled out to an old wooden fishing vessel and began helping the passengers climb onboard.

When it was Nam's turn, he stood up, but lost his balance in the rocking basket. He started to fall overboard, but then felt a strong hand grip him by the arm and haul him back. Nam and more than 40 escapees crammed onto the shabby 35-foot-long vessel. The Vos were the only intact two-parent family. Among the passengers were 12 children, many traveling with a single parent or a relative. Several teenagers were fleeing on their own to seek a fresh start and to avoid serving in the communist military. The rest were young couples and a few older ones.

Like many of the passengers, the Vos brought few possessions with them. The children had only the clothes they were wearing. Thu and Trien toted small bags of dried food, canned milk, and ginger for seasickness. Trien also carried documents that showed he fought for the South Vietnamese Air Force and was trained by the United States military—vital papers that would help him prove to United Nations officials that he was an anti-communist.

As the vessel chugged away from the coast and began to sway in the choppy waters of the South China Sea, Nam fretted with questions: *Will I ever go home again? Will I ever see my friends and relatives? Where will we end up? Are we in danger? What if the boat sinks?* Then he threw up.

Nam woke up later that morning to find someone sitting on him in the overloaded boat. He wormed his way through tangled arms and legs to reach his parents. Holding his stomach, which was roiling from seasickness, Nam threw up again, this time on his mother. So did his little brother, Long. Trien sympathized with them because he was suffering from the same malady, too. The ginger Thu gave them didn't do much good.

The vessel was heading for the dynamic city of Hong Kong, which the British controlled at the time even though it was in China. The 650-mile (1,046-kilometer) voyage was expected to take several days—if all went well on the unforgiving South China Sea.

Like great white sharks searching for prey, bloodthirsty pirates lurked in the waters virtually unchallenged, because the Vietnamese and Chinese governments didn't care about the boat people's safety. Armed with automatic weapons from the war and razor-sharp cutlasses, the pirates scoured the sea for easy victims to rob and murder. Adding to the danger, Vietnamese navy gunboats were cruising the waters in search of escapees to capture.

A few days out, the captain—a young man who was also escaping—announced that the engine had conked out, and they were now dead in the water. For several days, the boat drifted aimlessly, demoralizing the passengers. The threat of being raided by pirates or captured by the Vietnamese navy increased. Some of the passengers who were mechanically inclined tinkered with the engine and were baffled over why it wouldn't work.

Eventually, the captain confessed that he had sabotaged the engine. He didn't want to continue the voyage because he missed his girlfriend back in Da Nang. The lovesick captain admitted he was hoping a freighter or navy ship would tow them back to Vietnam. After an uproar by the passengers, he fixed the engine, and the journey continued.

Several days later, the breezy, partly cloudy weather turned menacing as thick clouds rolled in. The wind picked up, creating ever-bigger swells that pitched the boat up and down. Nam, who was still suffering from chronic seasickness, curled up in a ball and thought, *I just want to die.*

A typhoon gaining strength by the hour had overtaken the boat. Accompanied by shrieking wind, lightning, and thunder, monster waves crashed into the weathered vessel, drenching the terror-stricken passengers. Their rocking boat kept tilting to starboard and then to port, verging on capsizing.

As the tempest raged into the night, the darkness ratcheted up the dread gnawing inside every soul onboard. Convinced he would drown at any moment, Nam silently prayed.

Cries went up, "The boat is leaking!" Men scrambled to grab tin cans and plastic containers and began bailing water as fast as they could. Word soon reached the passengers that the captain had given up trying to steer; he was powerless to fight the storm, which was blowing the boat way off course to who knows where.

With their children huddled under cover in the bow, Trien and Thu, who were packed in with other passengers toward the back, wept. They shared with each other feelings of guilt over putting the kids in harm's way. The couple admitted that as bad as Vietnam was, with no hope of a decent future for their children, at least the youngsters wouldn't have been facing the likelihood of drowning.

"Why did we bring the kids?" Thu wailed. "We're all going to die out here."

"But if we stayed, we would all die another way," Trien replied. "At least we will die together."

They gathered the children and began saying the rosary aloud. A man next to them lamented, "What are we going to do?"

Trien shouted, "Just pray!"

"But I don't know how."

"That's okay," Trien replied. "All you have to do is repeat what we say."

As hope turned to despair, other boat people—many of them Buddhists—began echoing the prayers that the Vos were reciting.

After several relentless hours of fury, the wind and waves died down. When dawn broke, the boat was resting on a sandbar in an island bay, having somehow been swept by the storm past a ring of hazardous rocks without wrecking.

"How did we not hit all those rocks?" Nam asked his family. "How did the boat not sink in the storm? It's a miracle!"

"Without our faith, I doubt if we would have survived the typhoon," Trien told the children. "The storm terrified all of us, and I wish it hadn't happened, but we're alive. Your mother and I knew the risks of leaving our country on this boat. But we had to escape Vietnam because we could no longer live under communism."

"Where are we going?" Nam asked.

"Hong Kong, I hope," Trien replied. "But wherever we end up, it will be a better place to live."

The passengers had to wade and swim to shore, where they were met by Chinese-speaking fishermen and villagers. Because a thick fog blanketed the area and the vessel needed repairs, the visitors were temporarily stuck there. The islanders let them settle in an abandoned fort and brought straw for them to sleep on.

By now, the boat people were running low on food. Having hardly any money, Trien and Thu sold their wedding rings to an islander and used the proceeds to buy rice, vegetables, and fruit for their family as well as for others who had no provisions. As a special treat, the couple even bought rock candy for all the children.

In the village, Nam and Ha encouraged Long to sing for food, which he enjoyed doing. "Maybe we should trade Long for some fresh fish," Nam joked.

When Trien learned that the village had a shortwave radio, he transmitted a message to relatives back in Da Nang that the family was still alive.

After staying a week to complete repairs and wait out another storm, the boat people boarded the vessel—now freed from the sandbar—even though villagers warned it wasn't seaworthy. A few refugees chose to stay on the island, not willing to risk a pirate encounter or another typhoon. The Vos never learned the name of the isle, so they called it Seven Day Island.

After another week on the water, the boat people were rationing food. Each person received a small ball of cooked rice that tasted like diesel after fuel leaked from the engine and seeped onto stored bags of rice. Because of his chronic seasickness, Nam ate little. It was an accomplishment if he could make it through the day without vomiting. During the rare times he felt better, he joined children in playing cards, singing, and praying. Always praying.

The refugees were weary, hungry, and wondering if they would ever reach Hong Kong. Adding to their woes, their boat had once again sprung several leaks, forcing volunteers to take shifts bailing out the water night and day just to stay afloat.

One day a Chinese freighter approached and maneuvered next to the bobbing craft. When crew members saw what poor physical condition the boat people were in, they gave them bags of rice and other food. Seeing the scrawny, sunburned children, a sailor couldn't contain his emotions and burst into tears.

As the voyage dragged on, the endless monotony began sapping Nam's spirit. *Will we ever get there?* he wondered. Others had the same thought. But then, on the 27th day of their perilous odyssey, a cheer arose from the parched throats of the boat people. They caught their first glimpse of Hong Kong's Victoria Harbor—a destination that symbolized safety and hope. A navy cruiser motored out to meet them. Crew members transferred the women and children onto the cruiser and, while towing the battered vessel, transported them to an anchored giant barge that had been converted into a refugee processing center.

For the first time since leaving home, Nam felt truly happy, a feeling shared by all the boat people. No longer on the water or being seasick were reasons enough for glee. But the real joy came when he was given a bowl of savory rice with chunks of fried fish. "This is the best meal I've ever had!" crowed Nam. "And the rice doesn't taste like diesel fuel."

As night fell, Nam marveled at the spectacular view across the harbor toward Hong Kong's dazzling lights and soaring skyscrapers. Never before had he seen an urban setting of such vibrant energy, style, and color. In his imagination, it looked like a magnificent sprawling amusement park.

It certainly was another world—one that beckoned the boy to leave his past behind. This notion, that Vietnam was no longer in his future, was reinforced moments later when he glanced at the dock. He expected to see the waterlogged fishing boat tied to the pier. But the vessel that brought him to this haven—the one that had weathered storms and sandbars, slipped past pirates and gunboats, sustained leaks and mechanical problems for a grueling month—was no longer there. It had sunk, as if leaving no trace of where Nam had come from.

Safe in the refugee camp, Nam's parents were now free to tell him what they couldn't say while living in a brutal communist regime—that the United States, unlike Vietnam, was the land of freedom and opportunity. It was where the future for Nam and his siblings could glow with promises of their own making. And it was where the Vos were determined to plant their roots.

Trien and Thu met with immigration officials and applied for admission to the United States. During a meeting with an official who was involved with screening the family, Trien presented the documents proving his link to the US military and service in the South Vietnamese Air Force. "When it was clear that North Vietnam was going to win, I buried these papers," Trien said. "Right before I escaped, I dug them up and took them with me."

"You realize that if the communists had found those documents on you, you would have been sent to prison or even killed," said the official. "Why didn't you destroy them?"

"Because," Trien answered, "I knew that one day I would meet you."

Four months after arriving in Hong Kong, the Vos were approved to immigrate to the United States and were flown to a refugee processing center in the Philippines, where they waited for an American sponsor. During their stay, Thu earned money by making clothes and doing alterations. Nam sold the clothes at a flea market right outside the camp.

The family attended Mass in the camp every day. Nam, who sometimes served as an altar boy, became friends with a visiting Catholic priest, the Reverend Donald Staib, of Durham, North Carolina. The priest helped him with his English and talked about life in the United States.

After returning home, Staib arranged for Immaculate Conception Catholic Church in Durham to sponsor the Vos. When

Nam learned that he and his family were going to Durham, he tried to read all he could about North Carolina, but his source was limited to an entry in the encyclopedia at the camp. To improve his English, he read illustrated classics and studied a Vietnamese-English dictionary.

On April 7, 1987, slightly more than two years after the family fled Vietnam, the Vos arrived in Durham. The parish welcomed them with a furnished rental house, clothing, supplies, and food. Nam and his siblings started school while Thu found work as a tailor and Trien as an airport employee. Eventually, the couple started their own tailor shop.

Despite struggles common to most immigrants, the Vos adapted to American society and became naturalized citizens in 1992.

Once they perfected their English, the kids excelled in the classroom. As a straight-A student and soccer player at Riverside High School, Nam was one of only 45 seniors in the entire country to win the 1993 Morehead Award, a prestigious four-year full scholarship to the University of North Carolina. Later, after becoming the first in his family to graduate college, Nam earned his medical degree at the University of North Carolina's School of Medicine. Today he is a board-certified nephrologist—a kidney doctor—in Asheville, North Carolina, where he lives with his wife, Dr. Mary Beth Vo, a pediatrician, and their three daughters, Grace, Caroline, and Annaclaire.

Nam's siblings also graduated college and, like Nam, married their spouses in the same Durham church in ceremonies officiated by Father Staib. Today, Ha is a physician's assistant in

Winston-Salem, North Carolina; Hien is an elementary school teacher in Durham, North Carolina; and Long is an attorney. Trien and Thu, who still own their tailor shop, eventually repaid their friend who had fronted half the money for the family's escape.

"I don't know what would have happened to me if we hadn't escaped," says Nam, who has visited Vietnam twice since becoming an American citizen. "It's doubtful I would have had the chance to become a doctor no matter how hard I had studied over there.

"As an immigrant and former refugee, I have a great appreciation for the opportunities that are available in the United States. With lots of hard work, I was able to take advantage of those opportunities, which now have allowed me to do what I love— helping others through my medical practice. I will always be grateful to my parents, because they risked everything to give my sisters, brother, and me the lives we are enjoying today."

THE GATUMBA MASSACRE

JUDITH NGENA
Democratic Republic of Congo

Democratic Republic of Congo (formerly known as Zaire and before that, the Belgian Congo) is a country in central Africa blessed with natural resources, such as diamonds, gold, and copper. However, Congo is also cursed with a history of violence and government corruption that for decades has fueled hatred between ethnic groups and fostered human rights abuses, especially against women.

In 1994, the neighboring country of Rwanda turned into a bloodbath when the ethnic group known as the Hutus, who controlled the government, tried to annihilate their rivals, the Tutsis. But the Hutu regime was overthrown. Fearing retaliation from the new Tutsi-dominated government, nearly two million Hutus fled into Congo. Among them were thousands of the militiamen responsible for the genocide in Rwanda.

These rebels allied themselves with Congo's government and began to attack the nation's sizeable population of Tutsis, especially the related ethnic group known as the Banyamulenge, who had lived in the country for generations. Meanwhile, Rwanda's Tutsi government began supporting militias inside Congo that were fighting both the Hutu rebels and Congolese troops. Many Congolese viewed the Banyamulenge as more loyal to Rwanda than to Congo and, thus, deserving of discrimination and persecution.

The conflicts, known as the First and Second Congo Wars, dragged neighboring countries into the fight and led to the looting of Congo's riches. But, as is true in all wars, the civilians suffered most. Many sought refuge in nearby countries such as Burundi, Rwanda, Kenya, Uganda, and Tanzania. More than five million people died in the region—many from war-caused starvation and disease.

On a sultry June day in 2004 in the bustling city of Uvira in eastern Democratic Republic of Congo, 12-year-old Judith Ngena hunched over her desk at school, jotting down answers on her math final exam, when she heard distant gunfire. At first, she ignored it. But the shooting grew louder and more intense.

Not again, she thought.

Looking worried, her teacher went over to certain students who were Banyamulenge and told them to leave immediately. When she reached Judith, the teacher said, "You better go home now."

"I can't because my dad isn't here, and I haven't finished my test."

The teacher leaned into the girl's face and warned, "You must leave right away because you might not be alive if you stay here much longer."

Judith glanced outside. Banyamulenge parents were picking up their children, arriving in cars with mattresses, boxes, and luggage strapped to the roofs. Other parents on bicycles and on foot were collecting their children and hustling them away.

The crackling of gunfire echoed off the mountains that loomed over the city. "It's not safe here anymore," the teacher told Judith. "You should run home instead of waiting for your father. He might not get here in time."

Starting to feel scared, Judith hurried out the front door and was relieved to see her father, Osee Rukamirwa, hurrying toward the entrance. "We have to leave the city," he announced.

"Why, Baba [Papa]?"

"Judith, can't you hear the shooting? This time it's worse. The militiamen are coming down from the mountains, trying to drive out the Banyamulenge. Our best chance for survival is to go to Gatumba." He was referring to a camp that the United Nations High Commissioner for Refugees set up about 10 miles (16 kilometers) away, just across the border, in the neighboring country of Burundi.

"We're meeting everyone at the bus stop," said Osee, as he and Judith scurried away from the school. "We don't have time to go home first. It's too dangerous."

They soon met up with the rest of the family members—mother, Marisiyana Nabintu; brothers Claude, 22, Tubirore,

20, and Bisetsa, 18; and married sister, Nyakirayi Nyanzaninka, and her three children. (Her husband was out of town.) They brought with them a suitcase stuffed with two sets of clothes for each person and some bags of fruit and flour.

The family squeezed into an open-air bus crammed with fellow Banyamulenge for what they thought would be a short ride to the refugee camp. But about halfway to their destination, the bus was halted by an angry Congolese mob that had blocked the road with branches and rubble. They were stopping all buses carrying Banyamulenge.

"I can't go any farther because they might kill me, even though I'm not from your tribe," the driver told the passengers. He ordered everyone off the bus, adding, "You can walk from here."

That was easier said than done because the people in the crowd—including Congolese soldiers, Hutu supporters, and even children—despised the Banyamulenge. To reach the border, the refugees would have to walk through the haters.

As the refugees started their march, they were mercilessly harassed. Their enemies swore and spit on them, struck and kicked them. "Go back to where you came from!" the mob yelled. "We won't let you take anything out of the country that you bought in Congo!"

They began snatching personal belongings right out of the Banyamulenge's hands and off their backs and ran away with the items. They stripped the refugees of their jewelry, including Osee's wedding band.

Judith screamed when a woman slapped her mother in the face and tried yanking a bag of food that she had packed for the family. Marisiyana, who had a bad back, struggled to hang on to the bag as others from the crowd joined in.

Outraged by the assault, Judith turned to her father and said, "Baba, can't you do something to help Mom?"

"Honey, if I try anything, the soldiers will shoot me."

Claude couldn't stand to watch the attack on his mother and charged into the group of assailants. Seconds later, a shot rang out. Claude yelped and fell. Someone in the mob had shot him in the leg. Family members rushed to Claude's aid and wrapped the wound so he wouldn't bleed to death.

Judith thought, *We can't do anything to defend ourselves.* She was petrified that the tormentors would shoot the refugees one by one. *Is this how I die?*

They endured further abuse, but fortunately, no other shots were fired. Satisfied that the Banyamulenge had been hassled enough, the enraged horde let them pass so they could walk to Gatumba. Claude limped with the help of a makeshift crutch and eventually spent four days in the hospital.

Upset about the attack on her mother, Judith burst into tears. Marisiyana tried to comfort her, saying, "Don't cry, honey. I'm okay. The slap didn't even hurt."

Judith refused to believe her. *Mom is good at hiding things from me,* she thought.

Marisiyana had acted the same way—trying to minimize

a bad situation for Judith's sake—the first time rebels forced the family out of their home, which happened in 1999 during the Second Congo War. Judith had been a carefree seven-year-old living in the Banyamulenge village of Vyura. Even though Vyura had no electricity or running water, she was content. Her father was a teacher and farmer, and her mother tended to the vegetable garden. The family didn't have much, but it had enough. "As long as you have love, family, God, and peace, that's all you need," Osee would tell Judith. "Don't worry about money because money alone can't make you happy."

When Congolese rebels stormed toward Vyura, the villagers fled with whatever they could carry, leaving everything else behind for good. Amid the backdrop of gunfire, Judith and her family trudged for days, joining about 10,000 Banyamulenge on a dangerous trek out of the combat zone, where 250 civilians ultimately died.

The family finally arrived at their destination—the big city of Uvira, where they rented a large house. Osee was unable to land a teaching position because of discrimination against the Banyamulenge. To support the family, he bought cattle and butchered them, while Marisiyana sold bottles of fuel for lanterns.

The Anglican Church played a central role in the family members' lives. As third-generation Christians, they read the Bible after dinner and prayed before going to bed. On Tuesday nights, Judith attended church and choir practice. On Sundays, she would wake up everybody in the house so they had plenty of time to get ready for church.

Judith enjoyed school and learning new things, especially math. Outside of the classroom, she played with her friends until dark. Showered with love from her quiet, humble mother and compassionate father, Judith had few worries in her young life—except for the times she and her family had to hide or flee from militiamen.

In 2002, the Banyamulenge were under threat of attack from rebels in Uvira, so Judith and her siblings were whisked to the refugee camp in Gatumba for two weeks until it was safe to return home. Judith noticed that almost all the children at the camp were Banyamulenge, while her friends and classmates from other ethnic groups continued following their daily routines back in Uvira.

Now here it was two years later, and once again, she and her family were seeking protection at the same refugee camp. Located 3 miles (5 kilometers) past the Burundi-Congo border, the camp didn't have electricity or running water, but at least the Banyamulenge found shelter—and felt secure.

Most everyone assumed they would remain at the camp for a week or two until hostilities in Uvira had subsided. "I wish I had brought my schoolbooks so I could study while we're here," Judith told her father. "I still have some finals to take."

"Don't worry, honey. We'll be back home soon and you can study then."

"Baba, why did we have to flee? Why do other kids get to go to school and I can't?"

"It's complicated," he replied. "There are Hutus and Congolese who think that the Banyamulenge don't belong in Congo, even though our people have been living there for five hundred years. They think we are Rwandan and our loyalties are with Rwanda."

"Why didn't you tell me this before?" Judith asked.

"I didn't want to teach you to hate. I wanted you to love everyone, which you do. We are all equals."

"Some of my friends are Hutus and Congolese, and they are nice."

"Exactly, Judith. You don't judge people by the way they look or if they are from a different ethnic group. You judge them by what's in their heart."

The Gatumba camp was situated next to the town that bore its name, about 7 miles (11 kilometers) northwest of the Burundi capital of Bujumbura. Beyond the camp, the sparsely populated area was dotted with roughly constructed wood enclosures for cattle where young herders often spent the night protecting their livestock from predators and thieves. A vast expanse of marshland and grassy plains stretched to Congo.

The camp had a cluster of 14 large green tents and 1 large white tent on one side of a sprawling dirt field. Facing them across the field, about 100 yards away, was a grouping of 24 smaller white tents. Each tent acted as dormitory housing for several families. The green tents accommodated most of the 825 Congolese Banyamulenge refugees while the white tents held about 500 Burundians who had been exiled to Congo for political reasons before Congo had returned them. Because of a shortage of tents, a few Banyamulenge families resided in tents on the Burundian side. Among them were Judith's brothers Claude and Tubirore, who chose to stay on that side with friends.

In a tent shared by four other families, Judith lived with her parents, brother Bisetsa, sister Nyakirayi, and Nyakirayi's three young children. The family also was taking care of Judith's one-and-a-half-year-old nephew, Glory, whose father, Crispin, was Judith's oldest brother. Crispin and his pregnant wife, Jolie, were staying in Bujumbura awaiting the birth of another child.

Because there was no water source in the camp, Judith toted full buckets or gallon jugs from a United Nations watering station, a 10-minute walk away. Occasionally, she strolled into town with her parents to purchase food and various goods. Otherwise, she enjoyed spending her free time playing with Nyabyinshi Mahinga, her cousin and best friend. The two of them were practically inseparable, having been born two days apart.

Judith and her family regularly attended open-air church services held in the center of the camp. The congregation was led by Pastor Jacques Rutekereza, a tall man with a big smile, deep voice, and immense pride in his six children, ages 4 to 18. As a man of peace, he was a member of the International Action Network on Small Arms, which sought gun control in the region. At his services, the minister would tell his flock, "We must continue to pray for peace so we can get back home."

Amen to that, Judith would always say to herself.

However, hope of returning to Uvira vanished as fighting in and around the city persisted for weeks. Judith fretted that she had missed any chance of completing her final exams.

There was every reason for the refugees to believe they were safe at the camp, even though Burundi was still embroiled in a civil war, which was in its tenth year. The Burundian government was in charge of protecting the refugees. At the edge of the town of Gatumba, about a mile from the camp, was a small military base of 100 Burundian soldiers and a small barracks occupied by a few dozen national police officers.

On August 13, residents in town noticed a gathering of unfamiliar armed men in military uniforms of camouflage or solid green. When asked who they were, the men said they had come to provide security for the camp. Another group of uniformed men and boys carrying automatic weapons was spotted loitering nearby. Some of the boys were so small they were dragging the butts of their rifles on the ground.

Later that night, following the signal from a single gunshot, those groups assembled and marched toward the refugee camp. They were playing drums, ringing bells, blowing whistles, and singing, "God will show us how to get you and where to find you," and, "We are the army of God." They also sang choruses of "Alleluia" and "Amen."

Determining that these armed strangers were on a mission to kill, the police in the barracks began shooting at them, triggering a short but intense firefight. When the police exhausted their ammunition, they ran and hid. The intruders then continued striding toward the camp unhindered.

Unaware of the impending danger, Judith sat outside her tent with her cousin Nyabyinshi and a few other friends, engaging in small talk. Most of the camp's inhabitants were in their tents, getting ready for bed or, like her brother Bisetsa, were already asleep.

Suddenly, gunfire shattered the peacefulness. The burst lasted for several seconds. "Sounds like a Burundi farmer is at it again," said Judith, referring to farmers and herders who had a penchant for firing their weapons.

"He's probably trying to scare off a cow thief," said Nyabyinshi.

Then they heard singing in the distance. Recognizing "Alleluia" and "Amen," Judith said, "It must be the church people. But they always sing early in the morning. Why are they singing so late?"

The shooting started up again and escalated. Judith's mother hurried outside and told Nyabyinshi and the friends, "You all should go back to your tents. I'm not feeling good about this." To Judith, she ordered, "Come inside."

Annoyed by her mother's reaction, Judith thought, *Mom is being way too protective.* "We're going to be fine, Mom. Don't get stressed."

"I'm not trying to scare you, but my heart is telling me that you need to get in here right now." Hearing the seriousness in her voice, Judith went inside. At Marisiyana's suggestion, everyone kept their clothes on when they laid down on the ground on their thin camp mattresses. "You never know what might happen," she explained. "Let's be prepared." Marisiyana curled up on her mattress, wrapping her arms protectively around Glory.

Stopping 50 yards from the Banyamulenge side of the camp, the attackers began riddling the tents with bullets from their automatic weapons. Those refugees who bolted outside were immediately shot. Splitting into groups of two or three, the invaders stormed into the camp. They ripped open tent flaps and slit the sides, killing the inhabitants, no matter the age. Other assailants tossed incendiary grenades into the tents, which exploded in flames. As people fled their burning tents, the gunmen mowed them down.

Hearing frantic screams and anguished shouts, Judith knew the gunfire was coming from inside the camp. Seconds later, her mother cried out, "I've been shot!" She put her hands to her head and said, "I'm bleeding."

Osee kneeled by her side, trying to stop the stream of blood. But Marisiyana was losing consciousness. "Whatever happens, make sure to take care of Glory," she whispered, her voice getting weaker. "I don't think I'm going to make it. I love all of you . . ." She closed her eyes.

"Mom! Mom!" shrieked Judith, rushing over to her side. Osee looked over at Judith, shook his head, and said, "She's gone."

Those two words hit Judith as if she had been punched hard in the stomach. "No! No!" *This can't be happening. It just can't!*

"Get on the ground and stay close together," Osee ordered. When he picked up Glory, Osee groaned, "Oh, no! Glory has been shot, too! His shoulder is bleeding!"

Terrified, Judith thought, *Where can we go that's safe?* She peeked outside and saw bodies, illuminated by the burning tents, sprawled everywhere. "There's no way out!" she yelled. "There's nowhere to run!"

"Just lie on the ground and be quiet," Osee said.

Right outside the tent, shooters were singing, "Come, come, we're going to save you!" One of them slashed the side of Judith's tent and tossed in a grenade that touched off a fire in the farthest corner from her. The gunmen then sprayed the tent with bullets.

Judith's sister Nyakirayi began screaming hysterically. Her two youngest—Fille, three, and Felix, one—lay lifeless, victims of the grenade. Just then, a bullet tore into Nyakirayi's right arm. Using her left hand to grab the hand of her eight-year-old son, Bienvenu, she led him out through a large tear in the tent.

Seeing the flames, Osee told Judith, "If we stay here any longer, we will burn alive. We have to make a run for it. If they kill us, they kill us."

Judith picked up Glory, who was losing consciousness, and headed for the tent opening when she saw her father tumble to the ground from a gunshot wound to his leg. He bellowed in pain and asked Bisetsa to help him. Bisetsa then clutched his neck and began to go limp. Osee rose to help him, but the lad collapsed in his arms from a bullet that had struck an artery. Osee laid him down, bent over him, and covered him with a blanket. There was nothing more Osee could do but watch the life drain out of his son. Moments later, he lamented, "Bisetsa is dead."

It was another emotional body blow to Judith. *I've lost my mother, brother, niece, and nephew in just seconds!*

She looked at her father, whose pant leg was soaked in his blood. "We have to go," she said.

When they reached the tent opening, they encountered three armed men in military uniforms. "Come, we are going to help you," said the group's leader, speaking Kinyarwanda, the Banyamulenge language that she understood. *Oh, thank goodness*, she thought. *Somebody has finally come to rescue us.*

Osee lurched out of the tent with Judith. But their relief turned to terror when the men pointed their weapons at them and ordered Osee to drop to his knees and told Judith to sit on the ground. The leader glowered at Judith and hissed, "Watch what happens next. If you move an inch or say one little word, we will kill you." Then the men murdered Osee.

The three men casually walked off, leaving Judith too shocked and too numb to move. Her mind couldn't fully grasp the savagery she had witnessed. *This is a horrible dream. It has to be. Judith, wake up! Wake up!* Nothing in the darkest recesses of her imagination could create an evil this appalling. *This can't be real! It just can't.*

All around her, pandemonium reigned. The rampaging marauders were still shooting victims. Bloodied children were crying out for their mothers, and wounded mothers were yelling for their children.

Who does this? she wondered. *Are they even human? No, they are animals. No, worse than animals.*

The invaders targeted only those refugees on the Banyamulenge side of the camp. They did not attack anyone on the Burundian side, where they had posted gunmen outside those tents, warning the Burundians to remain inside.

When the massacre ended, several women collaborators, who had been encouraging the shooters with songs and cheers, helped the assailants haul away items such as money, radios, and clothing that they had plundered from their victims. As the triumphant gunmen paraded out of the ravaged camp, they began singing again. Their Christian songs and beating drums slowly faded in the distance.

The casualty count: 166 dead. Of those, 86 were children, including twin four-year-olds. The youngest victim was only three months old. More than 100 other people suffered serious wounds. The toll didn't take into account the emotional scars that the survivors would suffer for the rest of their lives.

Still clutching her unconscious nephew, Judith sat rooted to the ground in front of her dead father. For the next several hours, she just stared at his remains.

The Burundi soldiers and police officers near the camp had done little to stop the carnage. Commanders claimed they couldn't rush to the rescue because they were pinned down in firefights with the attackers. However, no soldiers or police were wounded or killed, nor did they inflict a single casualty on the enemy. They didn't show up at the camp until well past midnight, long after the murderers had left.

Police told Judith to leave with emergency workers, but she refused. *Is this another trick?* Judith wondered. *Are they going to take us out of here and kill us somewhere else?* She didn't dare trust anyone, especially the police, whose camp was only a 20-minute walk away. "Where have you been?" Judith cried to one officer. "You had to have heard the gunfire and seen the tents on fire. Why did it take so long for you to get here? You were supposed to protect us!"

An elderly survivor came over and convinced Judith to leave. "The little boy you're holding is bleeding to death," the woman said. "You need to get him to the hospital."

Judith and Glory were taken to a hospital in Bujumbura, where the toddler was treated for a severe gunshot wound.

Judith didn't realize until later that morning that she, too, had been shot. A bullet had gone through her right hand, but the pain had been dulled by the mental strain she was suffering. Unaware of the wound, she had assumed the blood on her hand was Glory's.

The boy's parents, Crispin and Jolie, showed up at the hospital, but Glory wouldn't have anything to do with them because he was so traumatized. The only person who could hold him was Judith, who was emotionally destroyed, too. She screamed, wailed, and clutched Glory for hours on end. Her anguish eased only when her brothers Claude and Tubirore showed up. Because they had been staying on the Burundi side of the camp, their lives were spared.

Although Judith's sister Nyakirayi suffered a bad gunshot wound in the arm, she and her son Bienvenu survived. When they had escaped from the burning tent, they hid in the bushes until the attackers left.

Judith didn't get a chance to attend her parents' funeral because she was still in the hospital. Osee, Marisiyana, and Bisetsa were buried in a mass grave in Gatumba with the other victims.

At the hospital, Judith spotted her Aunt Nyanduhura, the mother of Judith's best friend and cousin, Nyabyinshi. "Where is Nyabyinshi?" Judith asked.

Her aunt bowed her head and replied, "She didn't make it."

Judith learned that Pastor Rutekereza had been slain along

with six of his children. They were among the first victims of the murderers.

Whenever she spotted a friend's mother, she would ask if the girl or boy was still alive. If the answer was no, for Judith it was like reliving the horror all over again. She lost 10 family members—her parents, brother, niece, nephew, and five cousins. The deaths were too much for the 12-year-old to process. She wouldn't eat and barely drank. She cried hard and she cried often, especially when she saw parents comforting their wounded children. *I wish my mom were here to hold me.*

Her surviving relatives tried to console her. So, too, did United Nations officials who had come to Gatumba to investigate the slaughter. Even though they didn't speak her language, she felt their compassion. But there was nothing anyone could say to make the pain go away.

After three days in the hospital, Judith went to live with Claude, Tubirore, Glory, and his parents in a one-room apartment in Bujumbura for two months. During that time, Judith never left the apartment because she was too terrified that something bad would happen to her.

Not feeling safe in Bujumbura, she was relieved when her father's cousin in Rwanda opened his house to her, Claude, and Tubirore. He put them in school and paid for their tuition. Trying to make life as normal as possible for Judith, he encouraged her to put the past behind her and move on. But that was simply impossible for her. She had lost her parents and so many others. Without therapy—which she didn't get—she had difficulty coping.

Judith was wracked with guilt. She repeatedly asked herself, *What if I had moved and tried to stop them from killing Baba?* She suffered from recurring nightmares. Every time she closed her eyes, she saw the tents burning, the people screaming, the gunmen shooting. She couldn't talk about that horrid night even when her brothers asked, "What happened to Mom and Dad?" Every time she tried to answer that question, she went mute. It took four months before she was able to muster the strength to tell the story.

She had been a happy child who could talk to anybody, but not anymore. She was now a sad, lonely, reserved shell of her former self. School, which she had always enjoyed, meant nothing to her. She attended class but her heart and mind were elsewhere.

The only people she could really talk to were a few friends who had lived through the attack and had moved to Rwanda. One such survivor attended the same school. Occasionally, Judith would see the girl sitting alone with her head down. Judith would go over to her, and the two of them would hold each other and cry. Crying helped—sometimes.

When she was finally able to open up about the genocide, she asked Claude, "Why, why, why did this happen? What did we do to deserve this? No one should die like that."

"We will never know the truth," he said. "Nobody has been held accountable."

"There is no justice."

In 2006, Judith and her brothers went back to Burundi, but they never found the answers they were seeking. Unwilling to continue living in a region where blood was constantly spilling, the family applied to the United States for entry as war refugees. At first, Judith was hesitant about coming to America. She told her brothers, "I want to stay close to our parents' grave."

However, over time, she changed her mind. "Mom and Baba are gone, and we will never see them again. I want to go to a country where I can escape all this violence and never have to worry about genocide. I want to start my life over again—in America."

In 2007, Judith and her family were granted war-refugee status. They arrived in Seattle, Washington, where she started high school in ninth grade and quickly learned English. She was among more than 600 Gatumba survivors who relocated to the United States, Canada, and Europe, aided by numerous international governmental organizations, nonprofit groups, and volunteers.

She married Congolese immigrant Olivier Mandevu, whose mother and a brother perished in the Gatumba massacre while he was attending school in Rwanda. The couple, who live in Albany, New York, have four children, Benjamin, Daniel, Isabella, and Abigail. Judith's brother Crispin and his family live in Columbia,

Missouri, with brother Tubirore, while sister Nyakirayi and her family are in Dayton, Ohio, and brother Claude lives in Houston. Another sister, Nyamitavu Nyamasimbi, remains in Africa.

Judith works as a patient care assistant at Albany Medical Center. Olivier, a fiscal auditor for the state of New York, is president of the Gatumba Refugees Survival Foundation, which commemorates the Gatumba victims and calls attention to the ongoing human rights abuses and discrimination inflicted upon the Banyamulenge and other innocent victims in Democratic Republic of Congo and Burundi.

Days after the Gatumba massacre, the Hutu-dominated rebel group known as FNL (Forces Nationales de Libération or National Liberation Forces), which was led by Agathon Rwasa, claimed responsibility for the attack. As of 2017, none of its leaders had been arrested. In fact, the FNL, which was one of the last Burundian rebel groups to disarm, became a major political party in Burundi. Some of its members were appointed by the government to the Burundi National Assembly, including Rwasa, who was named deputy speaker. Despite the FNL's so-called legitimacy, some of its fighters have remained active, both in Burundi and in eastern Congo.

"Everyone in Congo and Burundi deserves the same basic human dignity and equality that we all enjoy in the United States," says Olivier. "We need to speak out and speak often about atrocities and crimes against humanity if we are to prevent further genocide. When genocide happens in one place, it is knocking on the door of the next victims."

THE KIDNAPPING

MOUSTAFA ALDOURI
Iraq

In 2002, President George W. Bush accused Iraq of being a threat to the free world because he claimed the Middle Eastern country, under ruthless dictator Saddam Hussein, possessed weapons of mass destruction. Although United Nations inspections found no such weapons, Hussein was, nevertheless, a global menace. He continued to sponsor terrorism and had invaded four neighboring countries in previous years. Over his brutal 24-year reign, he had ordered the cold-blooded killing and torture of tens of thousands of his own citizens.

With the consent of the United States Congress, President Bush launched Operation Iraqi Freedom to remove Saddam from power. In March 2003, the US and its allies invaded Iraq, starting with a "shock and awe" campaign of 1,700 air sorties that included 504 Cruise missile attacks on the capital city of Baghdad. In less than three weeks, coalition ground forces defeated Saddam's army, overthrew him, and began dismantling his government. The invasion led to the capture and eventual execution of the dictator.

The United States military occupied the country and tried to establish a new democratic government, hoping to give the Iraqi people the freedom to chart their own future. However, the process turned frustrating and violent. American forces battled insurgents, militants, terrorists, and ethnic groups that shared a lust for power and a hatred of the Western world. To complicate matters, many of these fierce factions attacked each other. The conflicts and ongoing war claimed the lives of as many as 3,000 civilians a month and displaced up to five million people.

Because Iraq was so fractured, its new government, police, and military weren't strong enough to quash the insurgents and create a safe and free society. As a result, crime soared. Among the wrongdoers taking advantage of the breakdown in social order were gangs of kidnappers who abducted ordinary citizens—between 5 and 30 a day—to collect ransoms for personal gain or for funding political or terrorist organizations.

To be home again. That's all Moustafa Aldouri wanted. For days now, the 15-year-old kidnapping victim clung to the hope—one that was slowly diminishing—that he would return to his family. Alive.

Shackled, handcuffed, and blindfolded in this terrible solitary confinement, Moustafa couldn't do much of anything but think. So he chose to focus on home, yearning for the day—one that might or might not come—when he would once again embrace his loving parents and sisters. Those warm thoughts did more than give him comfort. They eased, in a small way, his persistent aches from daily beatings and his constant hunger pangs from lack of food.

The beatings were bad enough. But this imprisonment was preying on Moustafa's mind and driving him crazy. Aside from the drubbings, it was the not knowing that tormented him the most—not knowing when he would receive his next beating; not knowing if he'd ever be released; not knowing if his family could raise the money to pay the ransom; not knowing the suffering his parents were enduring.

Moustafa wanted this kidnapping horror to end—one way or the other. He had made peace within himself, so he was prepared to die. Not that he wanted to die. It was just that he didn't know how much more he could take before losing his mind.

Born in Baghdad in 1990 to stay-at-home mother, Eman, and father, Mohammed, who ran his own mechanic shop, Moustafa lived in a warm Muslim household with Shahad, a sister four years older, and Shams, another sister four years younger.

During his childhood, Moustafa didn't fully understand the terror of living under the dictatorship of Saddam Hussein. The ruthless tyrant murdered or tortured real and imagined enemies—including anyone foolish enough to criticize him in public. He oppressed the people and rigged elections. To keep citizens from accessing the truth, he controlled the media and spread his own propaganda, especially the lie that all Americans hated Iraqis. He also forbade civilians from owning cell phones and satellite TV.

To Moustafa, Saddam was a powerful man, an admired leader—at least that's what children were taught in class, where they sang songs of praise with lyrics like, "Saddam, oh Saddam, you carry the nation's dawn in your eyes." But by middle school, Moustafa had learned Saddam was someone to fear. "Don't mess with Saddam," Mohammed told the boy, "and you'll be all right."

Most Iraqis accepted life under Saddam because the country provided free education, free health care, and enough basic services to keep the country functioning. Iraq boasted a low crime rate because the dictator was just as ruthless with criminals as he was with his political foes.

Moustafa never saw any violence and always felt safe walking to and from school or the soccer field in his mixed neighborhood of Saidiya. He played with kids of different religions and Muslim sects. No one asked if he was a Sunni (which he was), a Shia, a Kurd, or a Christian. It was never an issue. To Moustafa and his pals, they were all the same, sharing one simple aim in their young lives: They just wanted to have fun together.

School was important, too, in highly educated Iraq. Moustafa excelled in class, knowing that good grades would ultimately lead to a good life. The "A" students in high school had their pick of universities and jobs. As a fifth grader, Moustafa was earning his A's and had his sights set on becoming a doctor or an engineer.

In March 2003, life turned tense for all Iraqis when Saddam warned them to prepare for a United States–led invasion of their country. Moustafa and his family gathered extra food, filled the bathtub with water, checked flashlight batteries, and stocked the emergency kit. Every night, they watched TV broadcasts about the impending war. Daily reports said the United States and its allies—known collectively as coalition forces—were amassing at the southern border of Iraq ready to strike at any moment.

That moment came at 9:00 p.m. on March 21, when bombs and missiles began slamming into Baghdad. The initial attack was called "shock and awe," a military term describing overwhelming firepower designed to paralyze the enemy and destroy its will to fight. To minimize civilian casualties, the US targeted only military sites, electrical power plants, television and radio stations, transportation centers, food production facilities, and other "high value" objectives. However, as in any war, civilians were unintentionally killed and maimed in what the military calls *collateral damage*.

When the air raid sirens blared, Moustafa and his family huddled in the living room next to interior walls and away from the windows. Deafening blasts from bombs and missiles rocked Baghdad, creating enormous fireballs and mushrooming clouds of smoke. With every major explosion, the two-story Aldouri house shook as if by an earthquake. Eman kept praying that the family would be safe and that their home would be spared.

To Moustafa, it seemed surreal. Here they were, watching live TV coverage of the deadly attack that was happening right outside their rattling windows. Earlier, his grandfather Salman had obtained a TV receiver and set up an illegal satellite dish hidden in the house. When the power went out, Mohammed rigged the TV to a car battery so the family could continue to watch the attack.

"The earth is literally shaking in Baghdad," said one on-air TV correspondent. After the initial onslaught, a reporter said, "Large parts of Baghdad are already in flames." A third reporter grimly noted, "There is no safe place in Baghdad now."

Every thud from an explosion, every rumble of the house, sent a jolt of fear through Moustafa. *Will the next bomb miss its target and strike us?* he worried. The anxiety that held the entire family hostage eased only slightly after a second wave of bombing had ravaged Baghdad.

Despite Saddam's televised assurances that Iraq would defeat the Americans, few people believed him. Moustafa wondered, *What's going to happen when Iraq loses this war?* He hoped the country would change for the better—and that he and his family would be alive to see it. Several relatives were actually rooting for the US. "The American soldiers won't hurt us," a cousin had told Moustafa. "They will help us get rid of Saddam and make Baghdad like New York City." Moustafa didn't know much about the United States other than from impressions based on movies he saw such as *ET*, *Batman*, and *Lethal Weapon*.

While his parents took an optimistic view that life would improve, Salman scoffed at them. "You're happy about this invasion?" he asked them dismissively. "Well, you shouldn't be. Whenever a country takes over another one, things only get worse. You mark my words."

He's old, Moustafa thought. *He doesn't know what he's talking about.*

Three weeks after the attack began, coalition forces seized Baghdad, and by September, they installed a temporary government. Although the war flared up in other parts of Iraq, and suicide bombers and terrorist attacks plagued Baghdad, most Iraqis tried to get on with their lives.

Moustafa and his sisters returned to school, Eman did her daily shopping, and Mohammed worked at his shop. People were feeling relatively safe—and overwhelmingly pleased after Saddam was captured in December 2003. Iraqis started up businesses, were able to purchase cell phones, and got access to satellite television. "See?" Moustafa told his grandfather. "Things are getting better."

Except, in many ways, they were getting worse. In the wake of Saddam's fall, different ethnic groups and religious sects began battling for power, unleashing a storm of bigotry and intolerance against each other. This prejudice mystified Moustafa because his grandmother was a Shia and his grandfather was a Sunni. His aunt married a Shia and another aunt married a Kurd. "We were all mixed," Moustafa said to his parents. "Why should it matter what sect or religion we are? We're the same people we were before the war."

Hammered by sectarian violence, society began to break down. Compounding the problem was a lack of electricity, jobs, money, food, and medicine. Although Iraqis were free from Saddam's cruelty, they weren't free from harm caused by a soaring crime wave of carjackings, home invasions, auto thefts, and kidnappings. The woefully undermanned and often corrupt police force was ill equipped to fight lawbreakers.

Late one night in 2004, three armed, masked intruders broke into the Aldouris' home, woke them up, and demanded, "Give us all your money!" At gunpoint, the robbers stole cash and the gold jewelry that Mohammed had given Eman. "Call the police if you want," one of the gunmen said. "We don't care because the police won't be able to help you." The intruders left the Aldouris deeply shaken. Fortunately, most of the family's money was safe in a bank.

The home invasion unnerved Moustafa, but his father tried to minimize it. "This is normal now in Baghdad," Mohammed explained. "We should be thankful because no one got hurt. It won't happen again. They've taken our valuables so there's nothing more for them to steal."

The crime of choice for most bad guys was kidnapping children and adults and ransoming them to frantic families under the real threat of executing the victims. The money often went to fund terrorist and political organizations.

Moustafa was well aware of the rise in abductions. Kidnappers grabbed a four-year-old child who lived eight doors down and returned her only after the parents paid a hefty ransom. An 11-year-old girl in the neighborhood was snatched as she waited for a bus and was held in a room with four other kidnap victims until her father paid 5,000 dollars. Although she was released unharmed, the terrifying experience left her traumatized.

Moustafa figured he would never be kidnapped because his parents weren't wealthy. Besides, gunmen had robbed the Aldouris already, so what would be the point of kidnapping one of them? To be on the safe side, however, he and fellow students went to school in small groups.

One day in March 2006, shortly before his sixteenth birthday, Moustafa was walking with friends Hussein Ali and Mohammed Fahim to catch a public bus for school. They were unaware that an older-model maroon Hyundai Elantra had rolled up from behind and stopped.

A man in his late twenties jumped out, rushed up to Moustafa, gripped him by the shoulder, and spun him around. The man pulled out a gun, pressed the barrel to the boy's forehead, and ordered, "Get in the car."

Moustafa was so shocked and terrified that his mind went blank for a moment. When he felt the cold steel of the gun against his head, he shuddered. He flinched at the no-nonsense expression of the gunman and the stunned look on the faces of his pals, who stood frozen and speechless.

Should I run? Moustafa asked himself. *No. If I try, he'll shoot me.* As a sickening fear swept over him, he was shoved into the car, which was driven by a second man while a third man sat in the backseat. The gunman pushed Moustafa onto the floor in the back and made him lie on his stomach. While poking an AK47 automatic weapon into the boy's back, the abductor took Moustafa's wallet and cell phone.

I can't believe this is happening! Moustafa's terror-riddled brain began recalling all the horror stories over the previous two years of abducted kids who were murdered. *Am I going to make it or not?* He had never felt such dread.

The barrel of the AK47 remained against Moustafa's spine. *Oh, my God, any second a bullet could go through me and end my life.* "Wh-what's going to ha-happen to me?" the boy stammered. "Wh-where are you taking me?" He could feel the fear tightening its grip as if a boa constrictor were squeezing the life out of him.

"Don't worry, Moustafa," said the man in the passenger seat. "We're going to let you go real soon."

He knows my name! What does that mean? Are they really going to release me?

After going a few blocks, the car stopped. The gunmen stepped out and pulled him with them. "See, Moustafa? We're letting you go," said one of the abductors.

His comrade cackled and added, "Well, sort of." Then they stuffed Moustafa into the trunk of another car and closed the lid. The kidnappers in the first car left. Two men in the second car with Moustafa sped off in a different direction.

Near the bus stop, his pals Hussein and Mohammed stood in silence after the kidnapping. Even after the car was out of sight, the two horrified boys remained perfectly still. Breaking the quiet, Hussein said, "Mohammed, we have to tell his parents. Let's go!"

But Mohammed remained paralyzed, still unable to walk or speak. Hussein slapped him across the face, which snapped him out of his fear-induced trance. They sprinted to the Aldouri home and told Eman what had happened. Hearing the terrible news, Eman became distraught and collapsed, briefly losing consciousness. When she recovered, she called Moustafa's cell phone but got no answer. Then she phoned her husband.

The Aldouris didn't immediately alert the police because they worried such a move would infuriate the kidnappers and put their son's life at extreme risk. They also knew it was unlikely the police would, or could, do anything to help save their son. Left on their own, Moustafa's parents nervously waited to hear the demands from the kidnappers.

In the trunk of the car, Moustafa was fighting hard not to panic. *Am I going to live or not? What about Mom and Dad? What are they going to think when they find out I've been kidnapped?*

After a brief ride, the car stopped and backed into the driveway of a house. A man popped open the trunk and yanked

Moustafa out. "Don't look at me!" the man ordered. Then he punched the boy in the face. "Don't you dare look up!"

While the man used his hand to cover Moustafa's eyes, his accomplice roughly pushed the boy into the house and thrust him into a tiny bathroom. Moustafa caught a glimpse of an older man, handcuffed and blindfolded, sitting on the floor. The boy then tried to sneak a glance at his abductors, hoping to identify them.

"I said don't look!" one of the kidnappers growled before slugging the boy several times. They made him put his hands in front of his waist and handcuffed him. They also shackled his legs in chains and tied a rag around his head and over his eyes. *Maybe it's better that I didn't get a good look at them. If I had, they might have to kill me.*

After the abductors left and locked the bathroom door, Moustafa, who was woozy from the blows, asked the other captive, "What's going on here? Why are they doing this?"

"Shhh, don't talk, don't talk," the prisoner whispered uneasily. In a barely audible voice, he added, "If they hear us, they'll beat us up."

Breathing heavily from fright, Moustafa tried to get his fellow captive to give him any information at all. "Who are these guys? What do they want from me?" But the prisoner wouldn't talk.

The bathroom door opened. Moustafa could hear one of his abductors, Hasan*, outside the bathroom, talking on a cell phone with its speaker on. Listening to the conversation, the boy recognized the strained voices of his parents. In the foulest language imaginable, the kidnapper yelled at Mohammed and Eman and threatened to torture Moustafa to death if they didn't come up with the ransom money.

To emphasize their point, Yaser*, a brutal man who lived in the house with his wife, Namaa*, and their children, struck Moustafa. The boy screamed in pain loud enough for his parents to hear.

"If you want to see your son again, you will come up with a half million dollars," Hasan told the Aldouris.

"Are you crazy?" Mohammed shouted. "We don't have that kind of money!"

"You have more than you will admit," Hasan replied. "We know you plan to open an auto-painting shop and buy an expensive piece of machinery. We know where you live—you have a nice house—and where your children go to school. You have money."

Yaser hit Moustafa again, causing the boy to cry out. Then Hasan disconnected the call.

"How much money do your parents have?" Yaser quizzed Moustafa.

"I don't know, but it can't be much. My dad is just a mechanic, and my mom doesn't work." He yelped when Yaser slugged him again.

Lying on the floor, Moustafa tried to clear his head and calm his nerves. *How do they know so much about us? Dad hasn't told anyone other than family and close friends about his plans for a new shop. How do they know what school I attend? It's scary to think they've been casing us for a while.*

On the second day, Yaser came into the room and punched Moustafa. Then Yaser lifted the other captive and took him away. Moustafa never saw the prisoner again. *Maybe I'll be able to get out of this place soon like he did. I just hope I'll be alive when I leave.*

By the third day, Moustafa was starving because he hadn't eaten anything since his abduction. At least he could drink from the faucet on the bathroom sink. Later in the day when Moustafa heard Yaser leave the house, Namaa came into the room and handed the boy a fried kabob sandwich. As he wolfed it down, she told him, "I hate what is happening to you. I wish I could let you run away, but there are men sitting by the front door and they have guns. If they see you trying to take off, they will shoot you."

The next day, Moustafa could feel his frustration growing. He hadn't been told anything about the status of negotiations between his parents and the kidnappers. Adding to his exasperation, children were playing in another room, and Yaser and Namaa were going about their daily routines as if there were no battered, shackled teenager locked in the bathroom. Occasionally, he heard Yaser and Namaa argue, but he couldn't tell if it was about him.

Moustafa could count on one sure thing—a daily beating from Yaser. Sometimes the man used his fist, sometimes an object. Either way, the flurry of poundings on Moustafa's back, face, shoulders, chest, and legs left him numb.

Later, Namaa again apologized for the kidnapping and abuse. "Yaser is an angry man because he is hurting," she explained. "Months ago, one of our daughters was kidnapped and when we couldn't raise enough money for the ransom, they killed her. Yaser decided to get into the kidnapping business so he could find the person who murdered our child."

It was a sad story, but Moustafa wasn't convinced she was telling the truth. *I think she's trying to make up an excuse for his meanness.*

By the sixth day, Moustafa's body was weakening. He was losing weight, having eaten only once—just a sandwich—since his abduction. Suffering from the cuts and bruises caused by his daily beatings, he lay on the floor, unable to stretch out because the cramped space was too small.

When the bathroom door opened again, Moustafa immediately went into a defensive posture, coiling into a ball with his hands in front of his face, expecting the next thrashing. Yaser began pounding him until Hasan showed up and ordered him to stop. "Why are you hitting him?" Hasan shouted. "Can't you see what you've done? You aren't supposed to hurt him. From now on, no more beatings!"

Later that day, after Yaser and Hasan left, Namaa gave Moustafa another fried kabob sandwich—only the second time he was allowed to eat in nearly a week. Wasting away, the malnourished boy had difficulty consuming it because his body was slowly shutting down.

He hadn't given up hope, but he was losing it a little at a time. *How will they ever find the money? The ransom must be a lot or else I'd be freed by now.* To battle his depression, he pictured his release: the drive home, the emotional reunion, the return to a normal life. But those pleasant images were accompanied by a not-so-pleasant thought: *If the ransom is paid and I'm released, maybe Mom and Dad might not like me as much because my freedom cost them a lot of money. No, no, don't think like that. They would do anything to save my life.*

On the eighth day, Hasan entered the bathroom and told Moustafa, "We're going to let you go today."

Yes! Yes! Yes! Moustafa could feel the chronic stress start to lighten. He put on his shoes in happy anticipation of ending this dreadful solitary confinement. Then he waited and waited, but by the afternoon, his abductors still hadn't freed him.

Yaser broke the bad news to Moustafa: "You won't be leaving today after all. My wife's relatives came to visit, and we don't want them to know about you or that I'm involved in kidnappings. You had better not make any noise. If we hear anything, we will shoot you." He left, locking the door behind him.

Noooooo! Moustafa felt crushed. Raising his spirits only to have them smashed was malicious. *Am I ever getting out of here?* Hearing people laughing and chatting in the living room, he considered shouting and banging on the door to draw attention to himself, but he worried that the kidnappers would carry out their threat to kill him.

Afraid that his mind was beginning to crack, Moustafa felt he was on the brink of falling apart. Mentally drained and exhausted, he dozed off, wondering, *How much longer? How much more can I stand?*

Late the next afternoon, Yaser came into the room and took off Moustafa's handcuffs and chains but kept the blindfold in place. "Get up," Yaser said. "You're going home."

Is this another trick, or am I really leaving? Cooped up for nine days and weak from hunger, Moustafa could barely walk. He wobbled out of the house and was pushed into the trunk of a car. "Before we leave, we have instructions for you," Hasan said. "We are going to drop you off, and when we do, do not remove your blindfold. Wait until we are long gone. If we see you take it off, we will shoot you." He closed the trunk.

After a short ride, the car stopped and Moustafa was pulled out of the trunk. "Remember, don't look," Hasan ordered. "We'll be watching you." Hasan returned to the car and left.

Standing on the side of a street, Moustafa waited a full minute before whipping off the blindfold. Even though it was early evening, his eyes needed time to adjust from all the days of darkness. Looking around, he discovered he was a 15-minute drive from home. He flagged down a taxi and told the driver, "I have no money. But if you take me home, I can pay you then."

With each block that the taxi passed, Moustafa's heart beat faster. *I'm almost home!* When the cab stopped in front of his house, about 30 people were waiting for him. His neighbor, an auctioneer with a booming voice, announced, "Moustafa is back!"

As the crowd cheered and applauded, more neighbors poured out of their houses to greet the boy. Pushing through the crowd, Moustafa reached for his mother, who was overcome with emotion and fainted in his arms. With tears of relief rolling down his face, his father hugged and kissed him.

After accepting congratulations from neighbors, friends, and relatives, Moustafa went inside with his parents and sisters. "It's great to be home," he said. "I am so hungry!" But when he tried to eat, it was too difficult because of the condition of his stomach. He realized he would have to consume a little at a time. "I'm so grateful to be alive," he said. "When I was locked up, I didn't want anything other than to be with my family again."

The kidnapping took a heavy toll not only on Moustafa but on his parents as well. He was startled by how much they had aged over the past nine days. To him, they looked 10 years older. Their gaunt faces and sunken eyes told him that they had suffered from serious strain, pressure, and worry during his ordeal.

He learned that his uncle Sabah, Mohammed's older brother, handled negotiations with the abductors because he had the calmest demeanor in the family. He finally reached agreement with the kidnappers to pay a ransom of 20,000 dollars, which the family raised mostly through donations from relatives and friends. Part of the money came from the sale of the family car. A kindhearted neighbor added to the tally by selling his own car and giving the proceeds to Mohammed.

Right after his release, Moustafa stayed with his grandmother in a different area of Baghdad, but he was still apprehensive. He would wake up in the middle of the night from a nightmare, with his body shaking, and need several minutes to remind himself that he was no longer a captive.

No one really felt secure in Iraq as society continued to fracture and violence continued to reign. "We are not staying here anymore," Eman declared. "We must all leave for our own safety."

They fled to Damascus, Syria, where they rented an apartment and tried to carve out a new life. However, Iraqis were forbidden to hold jobs in that country, forcing the Aldouris to live off the savings that Mohammed had brought with him. Moustafa attended high school there and, during summer break, illegally took a job making purses, working eleven hours a day, six days a week for 100 dollars a month.

Despite his abduction, Moustafa missed Iraq and hoped to return there once the violence subsided. But it only worsened in lawless postwar Baghdad. Realizing his homeland held no future for him and his family, he thought, *I could do something meaningful with my life if I could live in a place where there is peace.*

To make his mark in the world, he wanted to live in a country where it was safe to walk without fear of being kidnapped or caught in the blast of a suicide bomber; a country where a good education and hard work offered the strong likelihood that he could achieve his goals; a country where freedom is cherished.

The Aldouris appealed to the United Nations for refugee status, not knowing where they would end up. After a lengthy vetting process that included interviews and physical exams, the family was approved for immigration to the United States. Moustafa knew then he would finally get that chance to do something meaningful with his life—in America.

In 2008, the Aldouris settled in New Jersey and set out to conquer the challenges of a new language, culture, and lifestyle. Moustafa attended high school and worked part time while his older sister, Shahad, and father, Mohammed, took jobs arranged by Catholic Charities (CC) in Camden, New Jersey.

After graduation, Moustafa attended Burlington County College (now known as Rowan College at Burlington) and toiled at three part-time jobs to help support the family. By 2012, he had saved enough money to buy a house that he shared with his parents and younger sister, Shams. He even started his own small business selling electronics at a flea market. One of his part-time jobs—acting as a CC interpreter for arriving Arabic-speaking refugees—turned into a full-time position as a case manager with the organization's refugee and immigration services program. He also helps American-born clients find housing and employment.

"Every time I look at my refugee clients I see myself from 2008," says Moustafa. "I know how they feel because I've been through it, step by step. I tell them, 'Work hard, because there is an opportunity waiting for you.'

"Refugees come here for a better, safer life. Once they feel safe, they work hard and then give back to the community, helping others. I see it all the time with my clients. After they get a job and work their way up to become managers, they call and ask if we know of any refugees who need work and then hire them."

The Aldouris all became citizens on the same day in 2013. "That's when we felt we were Americans," says Moustafa. "We have been treated very well here and we appreciate it. We are happy to be citizens of this great country."

RUN RAGGED, RUN SCARED

EH KAW HTOO
Burma

After a cruel military dictatorship took over control of the Southeast Asian country of Burma (also called Myanmar) in 1962, the government demanded its citizens embrace one religion (Buddhism), one language (Burmese), and one culture (Burman). However, many minority ethnic groups, like the tribal people known as the Karen (pronounced kah-REN), protested because they feared they would lose their identity and freedom.

Reacting to the protests, the Burmese army started viciously attacking the Karen and other ethnic groups that wanted to maintain their own language, religion, dress, and values. For more than 60 years, rebels of the Karen National Liberation Army have been battling government troops, who have engaged in blatant human-rights violations of Karen civilians, including mass murder, torture, forced labor, land confiscation, and destruction of entire villages. Fleeing violence and persecution from a succession of military rulers, generations of unarmed Karen have lived a fragile and dangerous life on the run, hiding out in the *jungle while their homes have been burned and their cattle and crops stolen.*

More than one million displaced Karen have sought temporary safety in refugee camps in neighboring Thailand. But these camps have turned into permanent towns for hundreds of thousands of Karen, who have clung to their long-held beliefs—many of them Christian—rather than return to a repressive homeland that has quashed political, cultural, and religious freedoms.

The dogs started barking. That's how six-year-old Eh Kaw Htoo knew trouble was heading his way.

The pets were the alarm system for the boy's Karen village. They never barked at approaching Karen, even if those persons were strangers. The dogs also remained quiet at the sight of any friendly rebels who entered the area. But the smart canines always let loose with a burst of warning barks whenever soldiers from the Burmese army were anywhere within hearing or smelling distance.

When Eh Kaw heard the dogs, he was dangling from a lower branch of a tree while his nine-year-old brother, Eh Kae Doh, was slightly above him. Although neither could see why the dogs were barking, their 13-year-old friend Kyaw Htoo, who was perched at the top of the tree, had a good look. Burmese troops were moving toward the village. "The enemy is coming!" Kyaw shouted. "The enemy is coming!"

The adult men in the village didn't need the teen's shouts to alert them. They were already on the move the moment they heard the barking. The men sprinted into the jungle to hide from the soldiers, who were on a mission to harass and capture them for slave labor. At the time, the military aimed its hostility more toward the men than women and children.

While the other two boys remained in the tree, Eh Kaw jumped to the ground just as the troops arrived. One of the soldiers pointed a rifle at Eh Kaw's forehead and said, "We heard you warn the village."

"It wasn't me," the boy protested.

"I am going to shoot you," growled the soldier. That was no idle threat. The callous soldiers had been known to execute innocent children for the slightest reason. Troops had been trained not to care about the sanctity of life, especially that of the Karen.

"Why would you shoot me?" asked Eh Kaw, unable to curb his trembling.

"Because you're lying."

"No, no. I didn't say anything."

Getting angrier by the second, the soldier shoved the rifle barrel into Eh Kaw's mouth and snarled, "We heard you shouting."

I'm going to die! the petrified boy thought. He wasn't sure what death would be like—he hoped it meant going to heaven—but he knew he didn't want to die.

Just then, Eh Kae and Kyaw dropped from the tree. Eh

Kae went over to the soldier and pleaded, "No! Don't shoot! He didn't say anything. Honest. He's my little brother."

The soldier ignored Eh Kae. Glaring at Eh Kaw, he bellowed, "Why did you warn the others?"

Eh Kaw couldn't respond. He still had the end of a gun barrel in his mouth. Even if it wasn't pressing on the back of his throat, he still would have been speechless. Fear will do that to anyone.

Seeing Eh Kaw on the verge of being murdered, his mother, Htoo Htoo, bolted from the family's hut, charged over to the soldier, and pushed him to the ground. Then she wrapped her arms around her son. Normally, her actions would have led to an immediate execution for her and her son.

But Htoo had learned how to talk to the Burmese soldiers to diffuse tense situations. Having grown up in the city, she spoke perfect Burmese and knew many government officials—attributes she relied on to persuade the soldiers to let Eh Kaw and the boys go with her back to her house.

This was the only world Eh Kaw knew—a frightening one where every day the innocent faced the prospect of being killed.

His world existed in a slender strip of southeastern Burma known as the Karen state, which the oppressive government divided into three zones. The Black Zone, where Eh Kaw, his parents, and three brothers lived, was a mountainous area mostly controlled by rebel forces known as the Karen National Liberation Army (KNLA). The Burmese army considered this a "free-fire" zone, which meant its soldiers could kill anyone they considered the enemy—even civilians. The Brown Zone was a rural area contested by the military and the rebels. In the more populous, safer White Zone, Karen were required to use a Burmese name and agree to a Burmese nationality if they wanted the benefits of citizenship.

Throughout his young childhood, Eh Kaw never had a permanent home. In fact, he never lived in any one place for more than a few months because his family, like hundreds of thousands of Karen, was always on the run from Burmese troops. The military constantly charged into villages in the Black and Brown Zones, snatching men—and sometimes women—and forcing them to work for days or weeks at a time as slave laborers, building roads, lugging equipment, cutting trees, fetching water, and carrying out other manual tasks. If they didn't work hard enough or fast enough, they were beaten. Anyone protesting faced execution.

The Burmese army ratcheted up the level and intensity of the attacks in the Black Zone. As many as four battalions would sweep into areas where Karen rebels prowled. The soldiers usually attacked each village with mortar rounds and machine gun fire. Upon entering the village, they harassed civilians by robbing, beating, and torturing them.

If the civilians were lucky, the rebels were nearby so they could rush to the scene and fend off the army long enough for people to escape into the jungle. Families often ran to hiding places that they had created earlier, where they kept a few utensils, a blanket or two, plastic sheeting, and a few days' supply of rice. To prepare for such raids, Eh Kaw helped his family cut bamboo, which they hid at different spots deep in the woods, where they could make temporary shelters if they had to run away from the soldiers. These basic shelters were concealed off seldom-used trails.

The Karen people planted vegetables and fruit trees in the woods and jungles so they, and future generations, would have fresh food when they went into hiding. To free their hands for carrying children, women often secured food, small bags of rice, and other items in their wrapped-up long hair.

Even after the army left the area, returning home was still perilous for the civilians. They had to tread carefully through the woods and jungle because the soldiers laid landmines on various paths.

Families would hopscotch from one village to another rather than go directly back to their homes. As a result, the Karen people were constantly rotating to other areas. Within a few months' time, they often ended up back at their original village—that is, if the soldiers hadn't burned it down. More than once, Eh Kaw returned to a village where he once lived only to find his home had been torched.

In the harsh life of the Black Zone, Eh Kaw was taught that his legs were the most important part of his body. "You have to be fast if you want to live," his father, Kyaw Myint, told him. "You must have good legs so you can run as fast as you can. Running is your survival because if you are slow, you will die. This is the only thing you need to learn."

Not every Karen fled. Those who owned land, cattle, crops, and wooden houses had to stay when the army approached. While the rest would flee, they were spared—as long as they bribed the soldiers with a pig or several chickens, or did a day's worth of slave labor.

Eh Kaw feared the soldiers for good reason. He saw things that no child—no adult, for that matter—should ever see. In front of Eh Kaw and shocked villagers, soldiers killed a man for using a hammock, which they claimed belonged to rebels.

Government soldiers looked for any reason to kill a Karen. Having a radio, a battery, or a certain watch often led to immediate execution because the military believed only enemy spies would have those items. One time, a Karen teenager who had studied in Thailand returned to the village to see his mother. When soldiers stopped him, they noticed his watch came from the United States. They figured he was a spy and shot him.

Had the soldiers known the truth about Eh Kaw's mother, Htoo, they would have shot her, too. Trained as an educator, Htoo wasn't allowed to teach in the countryside. But that didn't stop her from holding secret classes to teach the Bible and the Karen language. Even though the Karen were forbidden to practice any religion other than Buddhism, she defied the government as the first female Christian evangelist to preach the Bible in the Black Zone. The family had been Christian for generations, ever since Western missionaries began spreading the gospel in Burma more than a century earlier. By the time Eh Kaw was born, about a half million Karen called themselves Christians.

One steamy, hot day, Htoo, Eh Kaw, and other children were worshipping under the trees when a squad of Burmese soldiers sneaked up and surrounded them at gunpoint. Because they were either simply being cruel or waiting for orders, the troops made the children stand for hours. The frightened kids began crying. Eh Kaw had a tough time holding back his tears.

Hoping to stop the racket, an officer told Htoo, "Why don't you have them sing us a song? We will release some of them if you do."

The children started singing the only songs they knew—Christian hymns. But Htoo wasn't too worried that she or the kids would be punished. They sang in the Karen language, which the soldiers didn't understand. That wasn't a problem for the troops because they were enjoying the melodies and harmonies.

A young woman, Ma Pyo, whom Htoo had trained to become a teacher and a Christian, possessed a beautiful singing voice. She stepped forward and belted out a powerful Christmas hymn about love in one's heart. Her rendition, which she sang in Burmese, moved the soldiers so much that they released all the children.

Eh Kaw observed how his mother fooled soldiers with her acting skills. Because Htoo would be executed if caught preaching the Bible, she pretended to be someone she wasn't whenever she encountered troops. She would pass herself off as a lonely spinster or a person visiting a relative. To stifle suspicions, she and her family sometimes stayed in a Buddhist temple.

If someone brought into the village the body of a government soldier killed in a Karen rebel ambush, Htoo would cry over the corpse. Although she was sad for any loss of life, her sobbing was just an act for the benefit of the victim's comrades so they wouldn't retaliate. They had a tendency to execute a civilian—man, woman, or child—for every soldier killed by a rebel.

Htoo was so devout that whenever she lied to the military—even if it was to save her life or someone else's—she felt obligated to confess to her fellow Christians and pray for forgiveness.

In the mid 1980s, the military began ordering Karen in the Black Zone to relocate to the Brown Zone. Officers issued deadlines for the people to clear out of their villages. Most civilians waited until the last possible moment, leaving only after the soldiers gave them one final warning. Because of the decree, Eh Kaw and his family were forced out of one village after another.

One day, Eh Kaw and his little brother, Hsar K'Por, both in handmade shorts, were playing outside when the dogs began barking furiously. The men, including the boys' father, dropped what they were doing and dashed into the jungle. Eh Kaw assumed it was just another typical raid: A squad charges into the village, shoots guns in the air, and rounds up the men for a week or two of slave labor. But this time it was different. The gunfire was followed by a flurry of mortar rounds and rockets that were exploding here, there, and everywhere.

Rather than run away as his parents and older brothers

Htee Ler Doh and Eh Kae Doh did, Eh Kaw and Hsar slid into a bunker that had been dug behind Ma Pyo's home. She didn't need to run because she lived with her sister, who was married to a Burmese, which granted her protection from military abuse.

Inside the bunker, Hsar's shrieks of terror were almost as loud as the ground-shaking blasts. Eh Kaw felt like screaming, too. Ma suddenly appeared, picked up the wailing Hsar, and told Eh Kaw, "You wait here." She hurried off with Hsar as Eh Kaw remained behind, praying for an end to the bombardment.

After the shelling stopped, Ma returned alone and told Eh Kaw, "It would be too hard for me to care for you and Hsar. So I ran after your mother and when I found her, I gave Hsar to her. She said she left without taking you and Hsar because she thought you both would be safer here in the village. She didn't think you two could survive long in the jungle like your older brothers could. If the army chases after your family, she's afraid you two couldn't run fast enough, and that would put everyone in danger. She agreed to take Hsar after I told her you will stay with me."

The soldiers managed to capture several Karen men for slave labor and forced some families to relocate to another area. Those people who bribed the military with an animal or produce were allowed to remain in their homes. Ma and her extended family didn't have to leave because of her brother-in-law's Burmese status.

Several children in the village were left behind after their parents fled during the raid, but family friends or neighbors took over the care of the kids. Unlike before, when one or both parents ran off and returned a day or two later, none came back right away. A month went by, and then another without any word from Eh Kaw's family. *I'm never going to see them again*, he told himself. During the day, he kept sad thoughts from his mind by playing with other children. But at night, he cried himself to sleep.

Seeing the heartache he was going through, Ma arranged for a neighbor's seven-year-old son to accompany Eh Kaw to bed. Having a companion next to him eased Eh Kaw's troubled mind. After Eh Kaw would fall asleep, the other boy would return to his house.

In the Karen culture, the females cooked and tended to the fire while the males were responsible for obtaining the food. Despite his young age, Eh Kaw developed survival skills to help put meat on the table for Ma and her family. He learned how to turn bent bamboo and string into animal traps to catch birds, squirrels, rats, and snakes. Elders in the village taught him how to fish and forage for food. Sometimes when he was foraging, he would discover that the Burmese soldiers had cut down coconut and mango trees so the fruit would rot, depriving the Karen of needed nutrition.

Eh Kaw's prized possessions were a machete and a slingshot. He wielded the machete to cut bamboo, palm leaves, and firewood. He used the slingshot, which he handled with the skill of a marksman, to kill animals. The slingshot was the weapon of choice for the men because they weren't allowed to own guns. If soldiers caught a Karen with a gun, they would execute him and his family.

Although Ma and the elders were kind to Eh Kaw and looked after him, he missed his parents and brothers. But as time passed with no news about them, the boy figured they were dead because if they were alive, surely they would have come back for him.

About six months after the attack on the village, Eh Kaw was playing with friends when Ma came over and said, "Go back to the house with me. Someone is there to see you."

When Eh Kaw entered the house, he saw a skinny, extremely tanned man who looked vaguely familiar. The boy gave Ma a quizzical look. She smiled and said, "Don't you recognize him?"

Eh Kaw studied the man and said, "Dad?"

Kyaw held out his arms, and Eh Kaw rushed into them. "It's been so long and so difficult," Kyaw told him. "Your mother and brothers are alive. We've been living in the jungle, avoiding the army. We finally made it across the border into Thailand, where it's much safer. So now I have come back for you. I had to be secretive about showing up. If the military finds out, they will kill me. You and I will leave in the morning, and soon we will be a full family once again."

In celebration of his return, Ma cooked a big meal for the two of them—an entire chicken. At first, Eh Kaw was uneasy about eating all this food because his mother had always given each family member only a few morsels at dinner in order to get several meals out of one chicken. Now he was eating more than he ever had at a meal and happily stuffed himself.

The next day, Eh Kaw left with his father and two family friends. Kyaw stressed how difficult the journey would be because the jungle was crawling with rebels and enemy soldiers engaged in firefights. Eh Kaw had to keep a lookout for the Burmese troops in their olive-drab uniforms with a red patch in contrast to the Karen rebels, who were clad in camouflage uniforms with a white-and-blue patch.

Eh Kaw and his father threaded their way through the jungle for several days in a drenching cold rain. Often they had to hide from the soldiers or scurry in the opposite direction to skirt a firefight. The pair slept under trees and survived on roots and fish.

They finally crossed the border into Thailand where, at a small refugee camp run by Mennonites, Eh Kaw wept with his mother and brothers in an emotional reunion. Because the Karen rebels controlled the area and the Thai government left them alone, the refugees felt safe to move around.

Eh Kaw was the happiest he had ever been in his young life. He was surrounded by family and living in a bamboo house that his father had built. He was eating more food, including canned fish and more rice, which the United Nations brought in the biggest bags that the boy had ever seen. Eh Kaw marveled to his parents, "We have food. We have a house. And we don't have to keep running." No wonder he was so content.

Then Eh Kaw contracted malaria, which hit him so hard that he lay unconscious, burning up with a dangerously high fever for two days. A medic for the Karen rebels arrived and put him on intravenous (IV) fluids. After hovering near death for two weeks, Eh Kaw slowly began to recover.

Over the next three years, Eh Kaw adapted to life as a refugee, which, compared to how he and his family had been living in Burma, wasn't as terrible. He played and hunted and regularly attended church in a village where Karen rebels had set up an outpost.

Any semblance of a normal life—whatever normal was supposed to be for the Karen—was eventually shattered by the Burmese army, which held no regard for geographical borders. Troops began attacking the Karen in Thailand.

In 1990, when Eh Kaw was 10, Burmese planes twice bombed the village, trying to wipe out the rebel stronghold. Because it was no longer safe, the family uprooted once again and fled several miles farther into Thailand to a camp called Baw Naw, home for 7,000 Karen refugees. The family built another house and settled into a routine that centered on a Christian church.

Five years later, when Eh Kaw was turning 15, the Democratic Karen Buddhist Army (DKBA)—a renegade group of Buddhist Karen loyal to the Burmese government—triggered a fierce campaign of violence against the Karen in Thai refugee camps. After Thailand rejected demands that it force the Karen refugees back into Burma, the DKBA launched repeated raids on camps, which were scattered near the border of the two countries.

In early 1995, the DKBA seriously wounded seven refugees and burned down their entire camp. Then the intruders abducted hundreds of civilians, including women and children, to act as human shields to protect them against the KNLA on their return march to Burma.

Later that night, at another camp, the DKBA burned down 200 houses and destroyed 1,000 sacks of rice. As the refugees ran for their lives, DKBA soldiers captured hundreds of civilians and force-marched them across the border into Burma.

When news of the raids reached Baw Naw, Eh Kaw, his family, and thousands of refugees wondered if an assault would happen in their camp. They didn't wait long to find out.

Early the next morning, about 150 armed men from the DKBA, supported by heavy mortar shelling and cannon fire, attacked Baw Naw. The invaders then began spraying the houses with machine gun fire. Two doors from Eh Kaw, a teen-age girl was killed. He and his family raced to a bunker that had been built behind their church for just such an emergency. Soon realizing the DKBA was deliberately targeting the church, they left the bunker and dashed into the woods, where they hid for two days.

When they returned, they found the camp in ruins. More than 800 of the 1,000 houses had burned to the ground, including Eh Kaw's. What little he had owned was gone. But he was thankful that he and his family weren't harmed in the attack that left one dead and seven wounded. The casualties upset everyone. So, too, did the news that the DKBA had forced, at gunpoint, more than 1,000 Karen refugees back into Burma.

Like thousands of other Karen victims, Eh Kaw and his family, with the assistance of international rescue agencies, were moved deeper into Thailand to a sprawling camp called Mae La. On the three-hour drive in a convoy, the discouraged teen thought, *I'm fleeing from one place to another. This is going to be my life forever.*

At least he had the comfort of attending church services at Mae La. "We can't survive without our faith," he told his family. He loved listening to the pealing of the church bell—a sound he never heard in Burma, where he had to practice his religion in secret. Eh Kaw had planned to join the rebel army once he was older. But the more he studied the Bible, the more he learned about forgiveness and loving one's enemy. He no longer wanted to fight. Instead, he prayed for peace.

Although he felt relatively safe at the camp in Mae La, he wasn't happy over the strict rules enforced by the Thai government. Authorities fenced the camp in barbed wire and wouldn't let the refugees leave without permission, even if it was to hunt or fish. "We're kept in a cage like animals," he fumed to his parents. As more refugees poured into the camp, conditions worsened. Polluted water and a lack of proper sanitation turned the camp into a breeding ground of life-threatening illnesses such as cholera, pneumonia, and viral infections.

The camp did have a school where Eh Kaw first learned

about the United States and democracy. He wondered if he would ever get the chance to visit this country where citizens were free to worship, speak one's mind, and assemble; free to feel secure against arrest without probable cause and against unreasonable government seizures of personal property—freedoms no Karen had in Burma or Thailand.

In 2000, when he was turning 20, Eh Kaw saw his first computer and learned how to use it. That same year, he married Pa Saw Paw, a former classmate of his at the school in Baw Naw. Pa Saw had been living in refugee camps since she was three years old.

At the end of 2005, officials announced that refugees could apply for admission to the United States. Bursting with optimism and hope, Eh Kaw was the first one in camp to apply. But because of an omission on his application—he forgot to include the names of Pa Saw and their new son, Jubilee—he had to reapply. Time passed without any word, causing Eh Kaw sleepless nights and increasing frustration. During that period, Pa Saw gave birth to a second son, Jack. Eh Kaw wondered if his sons would ever know what it was like to live outside the fence of a refugee camp.

Finally, in 2008, officials gave Eh Kaw the only news he so desperately wanted to hear: He and his family had been approved for war-refugee status and would be welcome to begin their new life in America.

Eh Kaw and his family as well as his parents, two brothers, adopted sister Eh Ku Htoo, and their families settled in Georgia in 2008 with the help of Jubilee Partners, a Christian organization that assists new immigrants. "I have to think it's a sign from God that the group that helped us had the same name as my son," says Eh Kaw.

Five years after their arrival, all members of his extended family became American citizens. "We came here for a good reason—to escape oppression," says Eh Kaw, whose third child, Jessica, was born in the United States. "Here we are free to be who we want to be, and our children have a future."

Eh Kaw lives with his family in Comer, Georgia, and works for an aerospace company that makes aircraft parts. He says he doesn't take his freedom for granted. "I know what freedom means because I lived without it for so long," he explains. "Every day I never knew if I would live or die." He admits he doesn't like to talk about his childhood because "I don't want to pass the bad memories on to my children. I want to forget about it, but I can't. To forgive is easy, but to forget is not.

"I never had a home and never had a country. I always had to flee, so I felt like I wasn't a citizen of any country. But now I am. Now I am an American."

THE HUNDRED-DAY NIGHTMARE

KIZITO KALIMA
Rwanda

I n the early 1990s, the African country of Rwanda was rocked by a civil war between two ethnic groups—the Hutus, who controlled the government and made up the majority of the population, and the Tutsis, who supported or fought for the rebels, known as the Rwandan Patriotic Front (RPF). Under international pressure, the two sides ultimately agreed to a ceasefire and a power-sharing government.

However, before the agreement was implemented, an airplane carrying Rwandan President Juvenal Habyarimana, a Hutu, was shot down on April 6, 1994, killing all onboard. Although it wasn't known at the time, the perpetrators of the attack were actually Hutu extremists in the Rwandan military who were against sharing power with the Tutsis.

Hours after the president's death, Hutu soldiers, police, and militia began executing Tutsi political leaders and moderate Hutu military officers, triggering one of the continent's most horrific genocides. Blaming the RPF for the president's death, Hutu commanders decreed that Hutu civilians should kill every Tutsi in the country, sparing no one.

The Hutu population, which the government had armed with machetes, clubs, and other weapons for "civil defense purposes," had been primed to kill by an unrelenting propaganda campaign that led them to believe the Tutsis were their worst enemies. Following a tradition of blind obedience to authority, Hutus began a nationwide systematic slaughter of their Tutsi neighbors. Hutus even murdered Hutus who refused to kill Tutsis.

The RPF fought back. By the time the RPF seized control of the capital and ended the genocide 100 days later, an estimated 800,000–1,000,000 Tutsis were dead—a rate of roughly 10,000 killed a day. More than 400,000 Tutsi children were left orphaned. Fearing retaliation after the war, more than two million Hutus fled to neighboring countries.

Terror hijacked Kizito Kalima's mind—his whole body, in fact. Dark and debilitating, the fear had short-circuited his nerves and squeezed the air out of his lungs. This awful, overpowering feeling of panic had twisted his thoughts into a jumbled mishmash. The 14-year-old Tutsi couldn't think straight anyway, now that he was only seconds away from a brutal death.

At least the terror had numbed his pain from the blows to the torso, clubs to the legs, and kicks to the gut that he had endured minutes earlier from a violent squad of Hutu attackers whose vicious beating had left him squirming on the ground.

One of them yanked Kizito to his feet. Gripping him by the collar with one hand while holding a razor-sharp machete in the other, the assailant said nothing, but his wild eyes said everything. They burned with hate. Somewhere in the deep recesses of Kizito's fear-riddled brain, one clear thought surfaced: *This is it. This is when I die.*

Kizito's life didn't flash before his eyes. If it had, it would have shown the relatively privileged life of a contented boy. Growing up as the youngest of 10 children, he lived in a big house staffed by servants in a family compound that included seven homes inhabited by relatives, friends, and domestic workers. Smart and tall for his age, Kizito spent his free time riding his blue bicycle and playing soccer and volleyball near the town of Nyanza in southern Rwanda, an area dominated by his fellow Tutsis.

His parents, Denis and Cecilia Kalima, kept up a long family tradition of community involvement. Denis was a mayor, political leader, school administrator, and teacher while Cecilia served as a health advisor to the surrounding community.

Standing six feet seven inches and possessing a deep voice, Denis always made a strong impression, especially when speaking out against social injustice. Powered by his strong

Catholic faith, he earned a reputation for helping the less fortunate, Hutu and Tutsi alike. The Kalima household practiced what he preached, taking in needy young people at various times, regardless of their ethnic background. Teaching Kizito to love everyone, Denis declared, "We are all the same."

The Kalimas stuck to this philosophy, despite the personal agony of Hutu persecution in the decades before Kizito was born. The boy's grandfather was murdered by Hutus in the 1950s, and his father was imprisoned in the 1960s for anti-government activities. Upon his release, Denis couldn't leave the area without permission and was often under police surveillance. When civil war broke out in 1990, Denis recruited members for the Tutsi rebel group, the Rwandan Patriotic Front (RPF), in secret meetings at his house. Kizito, then in middle school, and his cousins acted as watchdogs and alerted Denis of any approaching authorities.

The civil war ended in 1993, but the bitterness between Hutus and Tutsis still simmered. Hutu Power, a new radio station founded by Hutu extremists, broadcast nonstop racist, anti-Tutsi propaganda, obscene jokes, and music. Recruits for Hutu militias practiced their skills with machetes by cutting down banana trees. The trees represented the Tutsis, who generally were much taller than the Hutus.

As one of only two Tutsis in a class of 45 at the all-boys boarding school he attended, Kizito sensed that his Hutu friends and teachers looked at him differently. They referred to his people as "cockroaches" and "snakes," common slurs hurled at Tutsis. One teacher told him, "You're a Tutsi, and you need to know your place."

In March 1994, Kizito was devastated by the unexpected death of his father. Denis had died shortly after consuming a soft drink at a store on his way home from church. The family suspected a Hutu served him the drink in a poisoned glass. Losing his father shattered Kizito. When he returned to school after the funeral, he couldn't concentrate on his studies and couldn't care less about playing the sports he loved so much. His heart was broken. When the boy came home for Easter break, he felt alone and depressed because Denis—his mentor, his role model, his moral compass—was no longer there.

Less than a month later, early on the morning of April 6, Kizito heard on the radio that President Juvenal Habyarimana was killed when his plane was shot down. *Good*, Kizito thought. *I never liked the man. He oppressed the Tutsis. Life in Rwanda should get better now.*

The boy bounded into his mother's bedroom, woke her up, and announced, "The president died! Isn't that great?"

Cecilia's jaw dropped, and her head lowered into her hands.

Confused, Kizito asked, "Why aren't you excited?"

"I'm scared," she replied. "Get everybody up and meet me in the living room."

He awakened his brother Benjamin, 21, sister Monique, 18, and two loyal Hutu housekeepers. After they gathered, Kizito stared at his mother, who was the toughest person he knew. He had never seen her so frightened. Cecilia told the group, "Throughout Rwandan history, whenever the country's leader dies, a Tutsi massacre always follows. Things are going to get bad. A genocide is coming."

Over the next few days, the family heard reports of atrocities against Tutsis in the larger cities. As the killings began to spread, Kizito's brother Egide, 29, and other relatives from out of town sought shelter at the family compound.

Kizito could feel the anxiety building inside him when he heard the Hutu Power radio station declare that the RPF had killed the president, so "all cockroaches [meaning Tutsis] must die." During pauses in its gospel music, Hutu Power broadcast ominous messages such as "Hutus must chop down the trees" or "Hutus must work against [kill] the snakes." Announcers were even directing Hutus to places where Tutsis lived.

Hutu militia, made up of trained and untrained civilians, and police mobilized to carry out the genocide, freeing Rwandan soldiers to battle the RPF rebels, who took up arms to stop the massacre. At roadblocks manned by Hutus, each passing person was required to show an identity card, which listed his or her ethnicity. The bearer of a card marked "Tutsi" was often executed on the spot.

Kizito was listening to the radio on the back porch when Hutu police barged into the house and held everyone inside at gunpoint. Scared stiff, the boy leaped off the porch, jumped over the back fence, and dashed up a nearby hill. After catching his breath, he turned around. He saw homes of Tutsi neighbors in flames and heard scattered gunfire. *The genocide has reached Nyanza,* he thought. *Did they murder my family?*

After the police left, Kizito cautiously returned to the house, afraid of what he might find. To his great relief, the family wasn't harmed, but the invaders had ransacked the house, flipped over furniture, and taken valuables. "They will be back to kill us, so we must hide," Cecilia said.

Benjamin and Egide left for the neighboring country of Burundi. Kizito, Monique, their cousin Jean Marie Kananura, 14, and his brother Concorde, 13, and cousin Adolphe Hotereshi, 14, hid in the home of family friend Aimable Munyaneza, 25, who lived in the town of Kigoma, about 6 miles (10 kilometers) away. Even though Aimable was a Hutu, he loved the Kalimas because when he was a street kid, they welcomed him into their home and helped raise him. Kizito was like a little brother to him, and Denis acted as a father figure. When Aimable was older, Denis paid for his wedding and helped him get a house and several cows.

On the group's fifth night of hiding, Aimable's younger brother, Jean Hitimana, who was in the Hutu militia, rushed to the house about 1:00 a.m. and warned Kizito, "People in the village know you're here, and they've called in the killers. Kizito, the Hutus are looking for you. If they find you, they'll hack you to death in little pieces."

"I wish I could protect you, but that's impossible now," Aimable told the group. "Your best hope is to return to Nyanza, where you have Hutu friends who might help you. Getting back won't be easy because Hutus are killing Tutsis all over the countryside. I can't let you go by yourself, so I'll take you on the safest route."

Hiking toward Nyanza, they saw tracer bullets streaking across the late night sky. Kizito felt alternating waves of fear and anger. And he had questions: *Why us, God? Why are we forced to leave our homes and run for our lives? Why are they killing my people? Where are you?*

Shortly before dawn, the group stopped and hid near a bridge that was swarming with about 50 militiamen. As the first rays of the morning sun peeked over the hills, Aimable scouted the area. He returned and said, "The Hutus are funneling Tutsis onto the bridge, then shooting them and throwing them into the water."

Kizito and the others tried to ford the river a few hundred yards away. But they were spotted by Hutu lookouts, who shouted to their comrades, "Cockroaches! Cockroaches!"

Machete-wielding militiamen quickly surrounded Kizito and his group and then punched and kicked them and knocked them to the ground. "Stop! Stop!" shouted Aimable, trying to shove the attackers away from the victims. "Don't kill them!"

Ignoring the plea for mercy, a militiaman raised a club that looked like a baseball bat and swung it at Kizito, trying to bash in his head. But Aimable threw himself over the boy to protect him. The club slammed into Aimable's arm, breaking it. Crying out in pain, he rolled off Kizito. "If you interfere again, we will kill you," the attackers warned Aimable. "Leave!" Reluctantly, he ran off.

The leader of this small Hutu group stepped forward, pointed to Kizito and Monique, and said, "I know you two. You're Denis Kalima's kids." Kizito recognized the leader, a man named Kanonko, who worked under militia organizer and Nyanza school superintendent Alyose Kabiligi. Years earlier, when Kabiligi was a teenager who was short of cash, Denis had paid his school tuition. But now, Kabiligi's loathing of Tutsis trumped any sense of gratitude or loyalty to the Kalimas. He, along with the mayor and police chief of Kigoma, had turned into Denis's biggest political rivals when Denis was alive.

The militiamen, who were thrilled they had captured a son and daughter of Denis Kalima, dragged the five young Tutsis to the top of a hill. From this vantage point, Kizito caught a glimpse of the carnage below. Bodies littered the bridge while other Tutsis lay moaning and dying along the riverbank.

One of the assailants made Monique sit in front of Kizito, telling her, "We want you to witness your loved ones die, starting with your brother."

Pulled to his feet by a Hutu brandishing a machete, Kizito could barely breathe from the terror. Too petrified to think or move, he watched the Hutu—whose face was contorted in hate—raise the knife high above his head.

Snapping out of his fear-induced mental paralysis, Kizito thought, *This is it. This is when I die.*

As the machete slashed through the air, the boy's survival instincts kicked into gear. He turned and ducked, hitting the man's arm with enough strength to change the knife's direction. The machete still delivered a blow. The point of the blade plowed through Kizito's high-top hairstyle and cut the left side of his face.

The boy collapsed. Like wolves attacking fallen prey, the militiamen pounced on Kizito. They beat him until he passed out. Hours later, he woke up shivering under a cold, light rain. *I'm still alive! They must have thought they had killed me.* His head throbbing and his body aching from the assault, Kizito stared at his soaked Hawaiian shirt, jeans, and bare feet. *They stole my jacket and my shoes!* Mud and blood caked his hair and swollen face. He sat up and saw he was in a ditch strewn with dead Tutsis.

But Monique was alive and so were their three cousins, although they were badly beaten. The attackers had broken Concorde's foot, bashed Jean Marie's back with a hammer, knocked out Adolphe, and stolen their shoes and jackets.

"We have to get out of here before they come back and finish us off," Kizito said. "Let's try to make it home."

They hadn't walked 10 feet before several militiamen leaped out of the brush and surrounded them once again. "We have the snakes!" the gunmen gleefully shouted. "We have the cockroaches!"

Kizito had reached the point of resignation. He was done suffering. *I wish they would kill us now and get it over with*, he thought. Instead, the militiamen forced the five captives to walk about a mile to a Nyanza grocery store warehouse where doomed Tutsis were confined.

Later that evening, Kizito and the others were taken at gunpoint to a grassy area where Hutus were executing Tutsis. *So this is where we'll die*, he thought. He began to prepare for his impending death. From his pocket, he pulled out a prayer card that his mother had given him and kept repeating the prayer.

Across the field, a Hutu yelled that he had spotted several Tutsis and needed help catching them. Distracted by their comrade's shouts, the guards turned their backs on Kizito and the others. "Let's run!" Kizito whispered. The five took off toward the family compound. Because of his broken foot, Concorde leaned on Kizito for support. Although that slowed them down, they managed to elude their pursuers because they knew the area so well. While briefly hiding in a sorghum field, they were spotted by a Hutu woman who Kizito knew was a born-again Christian. Rather than reveal the escapees' position, she told the militiamen she hadn't seen anyone.

When the five neared the family compound, they saw the houses were burning and flames illuminating several bodies on the ground nearby. Ordering the others to stay hidden, Kizito crept up to the corpses, recognized them, and then covered them with a large cloth. He scurried back to his group. Knowing how traumatized they were—and he was, too—Kizito didn't have the heart to tell them that those bodies were those of their aunts.

The group then went to the home of neighbor Anthony Kanyabashi, a Hutu married to a Tutsi. Although he was sympathetic to their situation, he told them, "I can't hide you here. It's too dangerous."

"Do you know where my family is?" Kizito asked.

"The last time I saw them, they were alive," Anthony replied. "They're hiding in the Seventh-day Adventist Church with other Tutsis because they don't think the militia will attack them in a church. You should go there. It's safer there than trying to hide around here."

The five sneaked their way to the crowded church, which held about 100 people, mostly women and children. Kizito found his mother, Cecilia, and many family members, including his married sister Emerthe and her two children. Cecilia, who thought Kizito and Monique had been killed, wept for joy when they showed up.

For the first time since leaving Aimable's home, Kizito felt the strain of survival ease slightly now that he was in a church with his mother. Cold, tired, hungry, and hurting, he just wanted to rest. A friend of Cecilia's gave him her sweater, saying, "It looks like you need it more than I do."

"Kizito," his mother said, her eyes welling up. "This is so hard to say, but you can't stay here."

Taken aback, he asked, "What do you mean, Mama?"

"The militiamen are looking for you. If they find you here, they will kill you—and all of us, too. You must hide somewhere else."

Just then, someone in the crowd shouted, "The militia! They're coming!"

Kizito rushed to the back of the church, jumped out an open window, and ran. Jean Marie did, too. They holed up a few blocks away in the partially constructed house of family friend Dominique Munyakayiro, a Hutu and born-again Christian. "Dominique would never harm us," Kizito told his cousin. The house had brick walls and only half of a completed roof. Exposed to the elements and unable to obtain food, the two teenagers curled up on the dirt floor and tried to sleep.

The next day, while peeking through gaps in the brick wall of the house, they saw militiamen and soldiers pass by and several Tutsis gunned down in the street. Kizito overheard one Hutu, who stood outside the house, boasting to a comrade about all the Tutsis he had killed. "I'm still searching for more, including that tall Kalima boy." From inside the house, Kizito caught a glimpse of the man and noticed he was a neighbor. Kizito whispered to Jean Marie, "How could he brag about killing Tutsis? He's married to one."

On the second day of hiding, the two were too stressed to think much about food or water. "I'm sick and tired of suffering, Jean Marie," Kizito said. "I'm ready to die." Hearing footsteps, they crouched in the corner, expecting a Hutu to shoot them. But it was Dominique, who screamed in surprise when he saw Kizito and Jean Marie. After hearing their story, he left and returned with a bucket of milk and a bowl of beans and ugali, a porridge-like dish made from sorghum flour.

The pair wolfed down their first meal in days. In addition to the food, Dominique brought Kizito bittersweet news: "Your mother has been spared—so far. I spoke to her and told her you and Jean Marie are still alive. She was so happy to hear that. She and the other women in the church haven't been harmed yet, but all the older males there were taken out and killed."

Early the next morning, before dawn, Kizito was awakened by footsteps entering the unfinished house. *The killers are here!* Kizito told himself. He prayed, *Lord, take me if you must.*

A voice whispered, "Kizito? Are you here?"

It's Mama! Flooded with relief, he helped her into the house. She gave him some food, a plastic rosary that glowed in the dark, and Rwandan money worth about 100 dollars. Because she needed to return to the church before sunrise to avoid being seen by the militia, the visit was kept short.

"Kizito, I won't be around much longer."

"Don't say that, Mama."

"It's true. My life is ending, but not yours. You will make it. I know it. It's time for you to be a man, to be strong. So many men in Nyanza have been killed, so you have to be careful. Take care of Monique and your cousins and anyone else who survives this madness."

The two held hands and prayed for each other's safety. "Now," she told him, "give me a big hug." He did and then watched his mother disappear into the darkness.

The following day, the mayor and police chief drove

throughout the area in a pickup with a loud speaker, declaring, "The war is over! Peace has arrived!"

Hearing the incredible news, Kizito and Jean Marie embraced. Their joy lifted the chronic torment that had nearly crushed them since the genocide began.

The announcement encouraged Tutsis to gather in the parking lot at the Seventh-day Adventist Church so they could receive help. Many Tutsis, like Kizito and Jean Marie, emerged from their hiding places and reunited with family and friends. Among them were Kizito's sister Irene and her seven children, including three sets of twins, the youngest only three months old. Cecilia, Monique, Concorde, and Adolphe were there, too. Many of the survivors were filthy and had lice in their hair. Kizito's face was still badly swollen and layered with dirt and dried blood, and every inch of his body hurt.

A small group of well-meaning Hutus arrived at the church, bringing milk, food, and beans as well as pots and cooking utensils for the Tutsi survivors. A short while later, authorities told the Tutsis, "You must follow us to Kigoma, where we will take care of you and protect you."

Protect us from what? Kizito wondered. *I thought the war is over.* But he was too weary to press the issue. With armed soldiers and militiamen walking beside them, the Tutsis began the 6-mile (10-kilometer) trek on the highway to Kigoma. It wasn't a pleasant march. Bigoted Hutu civilians stood on both sides of the road, jeering and swearing at the survivors. Many Hutus sang, "Days are good for Hutus and numbered for Tutsis."

Kizito spotted several insult-spewing Hutu teenagers who used to play soccer and volleyball with him. They had been his friends. Now they were yelling, "Hey, you cockroaches, why are you alive?" A few Hutu neighbors, however, shouted words of encouragement to the Tutsis.

With each passing mile, Kizito became increasingly convinced that Hutu authorities had conned the Tutsis; that there would be no humanitarian relief in Kigoma but rather more misery—and more death. He hoped he was wrong.

Outside of Kigoma, authorities led them to a hilltop warehouse to spend the night with Tutsis who had come from other communities. The Hutus then picked out those male Tutsis who were educated or locally influential—doctors, lawyers, accountants—and took them to city hall. They were never seen again.

Two days later, Kizito was milling around outside with other Tutsis when he spotted a long line of vehicles—pickups, cars, trucks, and SUVs—racing toward them. Hutus in the vehicles were yelling war chants and singing songs about killing the cockroaches and snakes. They were also blowing whistles, a signal for armed Hutu civilians to join them in a mass killing.

"We've been tricked!" Kizito shouted.

Screaming in terror, Tutsis bolted as the first arriving Hutus began firing their automatic weapons and tossing grenades. Panic-stricken, Kizito sprinted toward a swamp at the bottom of the hill. But a boy next to him took a bullet in the shoulder, fell forward, and tripped up Kizito, who tumbled and rolled onto a terraced area.

Kizito scrambled to his feet and jumped over a woman who was clutching two babies while crouched in a ditch. *That's Irene!* As bullets whizzed by, Kizito stopped and turned around to help his sister.

But she motioned him to keep going. "I twisted my ankle," she shouted to him. "But we'll be okay because they won't find us. Save yourself. Run! Run!"

Seeing the militiamen charging down the hill, Kizito spun on his heels and dashed into the swamp, where he concealed himself in a thicket. Lying down, he heard screams and shrieks, gunfire and explosions. Shortly after the bedlam quieted down, a dog barked just a few feet away from him. Kizito turned his head and came face-to-face with a growling hunting dog, its fangs bared. *It sniffed me out!* He looked up and stared at a Hutu who was holding a grenade and a spear. *Captured again!*

"Get up and get out of there!" the Hutu ordered.

"Don't kill me," Kizito pleaded.

"Do you have any money?" the Hutu asked.

"No."

"Then I'm going to kill you!"

Kizito remembered the money that his mother had given him. He reached into his pocket and pulled out 50 dollars. The man took it and then called over a comrade, who demanded the rest. After Kizito gave it to him, the two Hutus refused to let him go. Instead, they summoned more militiamen, who tied his hands behind his back and, with a gun pointed at his head, led him up the hill.

When they reached the top, Kizito saw Hutus cramming Tutsi women and children into vehicles lined up by the warehouse. He watched helplessly as militiamen grabbed his mother, Cecilia, and thrust her toward a small red Datsun. A gunman opened the trunk and tried to shove her inside. "Young man, don't push me," she protested. "I can get in by myself." He stuffed her into the trunk anyway and slammed it shut.

When all the cars were full, a gunman told Kizito, "We'll come back for you and the rest in the next round." As distant screams and gunfire echoed off the surrounding hills and smoke from burning houses clouded the evening sky, Kizito wondered if the genocide would end only when every last Tutsi was killed. Militiamen herded him and the remaining 30 children into the warehouse to await the return of the vehicles. Some of the kids were wailing; others were too petrified to cry.

Kizito knew they would all meet the same fate as him. It was only a question of where and when they would die. *We have to escape*, he told himself. *And we have to do it now before the cars get back.* When darkness set in, he looked out the window and saw guards sitting around a fire, getting drunk on moonshine. Some of them had already passed out.

Kizito told the kids, "The Hutus plan to kill us, so we need to run for our lives. Don't be afraid. If you get shot, you will die quickly, the best death ever."

They pushed open the warehouse's double doors and

streamed out. Kizito hurtled down the hill. Hearing shouts from the guards, who just realized the kids had escaped, Kizito tore past the terraced area, through a sorghum plantation, and into the swamp where ankle-high mushy clay slowed him down. He had been caught so many times before that he kept running deeper into the swamp until he found a dry, elevated patch of ground surrounded by sorghum. *This is where I'll hide out. But is it safe? It'd better be. I don't think I can live through another capture. Oh, well, I'll probably die from wild animals or malaria or starvation before they ever find me.*

Confining himself to this little plot, the lone teenager waited for the end of either the genocide or his life. To survive, he built a simple shelter out of palm fronds, drank foul yellowish swamp water, and ate wild sweet potatoes and corn. He passed the time by reciting the rosary dozens of times a day through torrential rainstorms and in steaming temperatures of 100-plus degrees. The fear of capture frayed his nerves. Every strange sound made him suspect Hutus were close to him. They usually were, because they were combing the area for Tutsis.

After nearly eight weeks of loneliness, Kizito rejoiced when his cousins Vincent Kamugisha and Jean Marie, who had been hiding elsewhere in the swamp, stumbled upon him. The pair stayed with Kizito, whose health was failing. He was suffering from malnutrition, insect bites, hearing loss, blurry eyesight, and an infection that cost him his toenails.

One day about a month later, the three teenagers heard someone with a portable loudspeaker announce, "This is the RPF. The war is over. To all Tutsis, it is safe to come out of hiding."

Kizito didn't believe any of it. He warned his cousins, "This is a Hutu trick. They've done this before."

"I'm going to see if they really are the RPF," said Vincent, the healthiest of the three. "If they're not, well, I'll probably die in the swamp anyway. I have nothing to lose." He left and returned a short while later with word that the RPF had defeated the Hutus and secured the area. But Kizito was too weak to walk out of the swamp on his own. RPF soldiers used a wheelbarrow to bring him to a field hospital, where a medic gave him an IV, food, water, and medicine.

When Kizito recovered, he went to a refugee camp. On the way there, he passed constant reminders of the genocide— charred remains of neighbors' houses, bullet holes on sides of buildings, crosses and memorials marking executions of Tutsis. Troubled and depressed, he told himself, *I wish I were dead.* His grief intensified when his suspicions were confirmed: Hutus had murdered his mother, Emerthe, Irene, and six of Irene's seven children outside city hall and buried them in a mass grave with hundreds of other slain Tutsis. His sister Monique had survived, but she had become so emotionally distressed that she could barely function. Kizito had difficulty sleeping. Every night, he experienced the same frightening nightmare: the fleeing, the captures, the beatings.

Trying to get on with his life, Kizito returned to boarding school. But to him, it seemed more like an orphanage. His Tutsi friends either were dead or had lost their parents in the genocide. Even harder, he was attending class with students whose fathers had killed hundreds, if not thousands, of his people. It was just too hard for him to cope. Kizito turned into a surly, angry teenager who didn't care about anything or anybody—including himself. He spoke with his fists one too many times and was kicked out of school.

At 16, he was homeless with nowhere to go. The country smelled of death, a lingering stench that, with every breath, reminded him of the hundreds of thousands of slaughtered Tutsis. *Get out of Rwanda,* he told himself. He sought help from his good friend Aimable. After learning that a certain Hutu had stolen the Kalimas' cows during the genocide, Kizito and Aimable went to the thief and took three cows. "If you try to stop me, I will kill you," Kizito warned the Hutu, who didn't resist. After selling the cows to a butcher for about 300 dollars, Kizito used part of the money to pay for a passport.

Because he was tall and athletic, he bummed around surrounding African countries, Kenya, Uganda, and Tanzania, playing semipro basketball. Kizito earned barely enough to live. But he needed to play because the basketball court was the only place where he wasn't haunted by horrific memories of the genocide.

Other than hoops, he had no focus and no plans for the future. Then one day in 1998, when he was 19, Kizito received a letter that changed his life. It invited him to play in an international junior basketball tournament in Georgia. He accepted. Soon after arriving in the United States, he knew this would be his forever home. Kizito applied for, and received, political asylum as a Rwandan war refugee.

Finding comfort and security in a country built on ethnic diversity, he plotted a course for his future. Sure, it wouldn't be easy for a young, emotionally scarred refugee with few resources and no family in America, but he was not discouraged. Compared to what he had suffered during the genocide, Kizito figured that reaching his goals would be a slam dunk.

After living with foster families, Kizito graduated from Providence St. Mel High School in Chicago. He attended Indiana University-South Bend, where he played basketball and earned a degree in criminal justice. He then worked in the social services field in Indiana as a juvenile detention counselor, community case manager, and probation and parole officer.

For years, Kizito suffered from anxiety, depression, and post-traumatic stress disorder. He yearned for revenge against the Hutu killers. Through therapy, however, he learned to forgive. He's now founder and executive director of the Peace Center for Forgiveness and Reconciliation in Indianapolis. The center provides support and fosters healing for young people who have experienced the pain of injustice or other traumatic events. It also offers conflict resolution training, character building, and mentoring from caring adults.

"I survived because I believe God has a plan for me—and part

of that plan is teaching forgiveness," says Kizito. He has lectured at the United Nations and speaks at schools, churches, and community gatherings about ways for victims to overcome violence and hatred. "It's not easy to forgive," he admits. "You have to work at it every day. In fact, it took me twelve years to learn to forgive. And only then could I start to heal."

Kizito and his American-born wife, Stacey, have three daughters, Kayza and Rwandan-born Josiane and Liliane, whom the couple adopted. Kizito hopes to receive his citizenship in 2017.

WHEN DEATH CAME TO TOWN

ADENAH BAYOH
Liberia

As Africa's first and oldest republic, Liberia was established with the help of freed American slaves and declared its independence in 1847. But over time, political tensions grew as the government ignored or discriminated against tribal groups. In December 1989, rebel forces led by Charles Taylor launched a violent uprising to oust President Samuel Doe, who had seized power in an armed coup years earlier.

Flaring into one of the continent's bloodiest civil wars, the conflict fanned ethnic hatred to such a fever pitch that government troops and rebels began killing innocent civilians by the tens of thousands, depending on their tribes and which side they supported. As one expert said at the time, "It is ironic that the rebel factions that claimed to want an end to the anarchy in Liberia caused by Doe's army have themselves been inflicting needless suffering on the civilian populace they claimed to represent." Adding to the insanity, the rebels split into factions and fought each other, too.

By the end of 1990, Doe was captured and killed. But the civil war raged on until a peace accord was reached in 1995. The fighting claimed the lives of 200,000 victims and caused more than one million citizens to flee to refugee camps in neighboring countries. Liberia's economy was left in tatters, homes and buildings had been looted and destroyed, and offices and businesses had shut down. In 1997, Taylor was elected president, but two years later, the country was ravaged by a second civil war that didn't end until 2003, following his resignation.

Twelve-year-old Adenah Bayoh sensed war was in the air. During the Christmas holidays in 1989, she heard grown-ups in her small town of Foya talking about the rebels' storming of Liberia's capital city of Monrovia.

Adenah couldn't imagine any reason why rebels or government troops would swoop into Foya, which was tucked in the far northern corner of Liberia. The small town of 1,500 people certainly wasn't a hotbed of political turmoil. Nothing much interesting happened here except for the Saturday market, when farmers, basket weavers, and seamstresses came from the surrounding area to sell and trade their goods.

Most of the inhabitants of Foya supported whoever had the power in town, which, in their case, were the police and government officials. If the rebels took over, then most of the townspeople said they would support them. People knew that was the rule they needed to follow to survive.

Despite all this talk of war, Adenah felt secure because she knew her grandmother Jenneh Viskinda, who was raising the girl, would never let anything bad happen to her.

Everyone called Jenneh "Big Ma." It wasn't because she was a large woman—quite the opposite; she was somewhat short and sturdy. Big Ma earned the nickname because she was a woman of stature, one who commanded respect by her dignified, quiet manner. With her piercing, wide eyes and her flair for wearing colorful African garb, she always made her presence known.

In an age and society where women were expected to defer to men, Big Ma was a strong feminist and a sharp businesswoman. When her husband died in 1976, she raised five girls on her own and took control of the family farm over the objections of male relatives who felt they should have inherited it. Big Ma owned and operated a bakery, restaurant, and 50-acre farm that harvested rice, coffee, and cocoa beans. She also ran a wholesale business and held real estate. With her encouragement and guidance, she inspired other women in Foya to start their own businesses.

Adenah lived with her grandmother and several cousins in a large house, which was made of clay bricks and had a sprawling veranda that doubled as a restaurant. The aroma of baked bread wafted from a huge wood-burning oven made of hardened mud in an outdoor kitchen in the back. The house teemed with life because family members of all ages were constantly running in and out. The living room, which was tastefully decorated with handmade furniture, featured only one picture on the wall—an outsized photo of United States president John F. Kennedy.

Adenah, who wore American-style clothes rather than African, walked about 5 miles (8 kilometers) to school each way. She loved learning. No subject meant more to the girl than the basics of business, which Big Ma eagerly taught her from the time she was six years old.

The family home stood across the street from the marketplace in the center of town. Adenah loved Saturdays, when she joined Big Ma and scores of sellers who hawked their goods and produce from a maze of wooden stalls. This was Adenah's time to shine—and earn money. She loved to compete with her older cousins over who could sell the most bread, most cups of rice, or most coffee beans. Rarely did Adenah get outsold.

Big Ma's acquaintances from the outlying area often stored their possessions in her house before shopping or setting up their stalls. One market day, a woman asked to use the bathroom, so Adenah took her around the back to the outhouse. When the woman came out, she gave Adenah 25 cents. Being the resourceful girl she was, Adenah began charging other shoppers 25 cents to use the family's bathroom—that is, until Big Ma put a stop to it.

Adenah noticed that by early 1990, the people's joyous feelings on market day had dwindled into a more reserved mood. All anyone talked about was the civil war and when it would reach their peaceful town. Each passing day brought the conflict closer.

Tension mounted with news that the rebels—fighters of Charles Taylor and his National Patriotic Front of Liberia (NPFL)—had swarmed into Kolahun, a village only 12 miles (20 kilometers) away. Fearing bloodshed, some locals were packing up what they could and leaving for the safety of the neighboring country of Sierra Leone.

But others, like Big Ma, insisted on sticking to the routine of their daily lives, so when Saturday rolled around, the marketplace was open for business as usual. There were fewer customers than normal, which bothered Adenah because it meant she would make less money. By late afternoon, when the number of shoppers had thinned out, she was staring at a tray of unsold bread that would soon turn stale. For a girl proud of her ability to sell, that was not a pretty sight. With her grandmother's permission, Adenah slashed the price of the bread in half and managed to sell it all.

Before she had time to gloat, however, she heard a rumbling sound that grew increasingly loud. Stepping out from behind her stall, she looked down the main dirt road. Trailing billowing clouds of dust, a speeding convoy of cars, pickups, vans, SUVs, and half-ton trucks—all carrying men wielding weapons—roared into Foya. Some of the occupants fired their guns in the air to announce their arrival.

"The rebels are here!" shouted Big Ma. "'Denah, gather your cousins and get in the house! Now!"

Women and children—many screaming in terror—bolted from their marketplace stalls and ran in all directions. The caravan split in two. Half the rebels zoomed through town toward the police station while the rest stopped near the market and poured out of their vehicles.

Adenah, her cousins, Big Ma, and others made it safely into the house. But one of her aunts, Theresa Sheky, wasn't quick enough. She stopped and froze.

Peeking out through the curtains of the front room, Adenah and her family watched as a rebel strode over to Theresa, said something to her, and then struck her with the butt of his rifle. Theresa tumbled to the ground. The rebel stood over her and, using his weapon as a club, continued to beat her.

"He's going to kill her!" Adenah shrieked. "He's going to kill her! He's going to kill her!"

"No he isn't!" Big Ma vowed. She stormed out of the house and, followed by several other women, rushed over to the attacker and demanded, then begged, for a halt to the assault. He ignored Big Ma and the women. They tried lunging at him but he just shoved them out of the way. Several rebels formed a semicircle around the scene and passively observed the beating without trying to stop it.

From inside the house, Adenah could barely look,

convinced that she was witnessing the murder of her sweet aunt. *This can't be happening! When will it stop?*

As the brutal assault on Theresa continued, Big Ma resorted to an outrageously desperate measure—she began stripping off her own clothes. Following her lead, the women with her began taking off their clothes, too.

It took a moment before Adenah realized why Big Ma and the women were doing this. As Kissi people—an ethnic African group—they followed certain traditions and customs. One of these principles was that it was forbidden for a man to see an older woman naked.

Suddenly, the rebels, who had refused to interfere with the beating, covered their eyes and yelled at their comrade, "Stop! Stop!" He looked up. Seeing the half-naked women in front of him, the shocked rebel immediately halted his attack and backed away.

Big Ma and the other women put their clothes back on and carried the battered and bruised Theresa into the house. Adenah grabbed some towels, wet them, and gave them to Big Ma to help stem the bleeding. As bad as Theresa looked, she hadn't suffered any broken bones.

From the middle of the street, the commander of the group of rebels shouted out to the townspeople, "What just happened here is wrong. We are not here to hurt you civilians. As long as you are not a supporter of President Doe, no harm will come to you. But if we find out you are working for the government, say your prayers because you will not be long for this world."

A short while later, a family friend came into the house and announced, "The rebels went to the police station and killed the police. They opened up the cells and tried to recruit the prisoners. Anyone who didn't join the rebels was shot."

Big Ma insisted that Adenah and her cousins remain in the house during the siege, which had emptied the streets of most citizens. Over the next several days, the rebels barged into different homes, demanding to know the owners' loyalties. If the NPFL found evidence that the person or family supported the government, they were tortured and usually killed. The rebels tried pitting neighbor against neighbor, promising those who cooperated with good-paying jobs or positions of power once Charles Taylor took control of the government. Those pledges spurred people to spy on their friends.

For days, Adenah heard sporadic gunfire, always wondering if that was a warning shot or an execution. Whenever she peeked out the window, she often witnessed rebels thrashing or torturing someone and leaving them to die. However horrible it was for her to watch, the worst part was recognizing that the victim was a neighbor, a family acquaintance, or a worker she knew.

"The rebels want us to notice all the evil they can do because they are trying to terrorize us," Big Ma said. "They are leaving us a message."

The girl felt numb from seeing all this violence. Every day, she woke up with the same stomach-churning thought: *Are we*

*going to be next? Is someone going to lie and say Grandma is sup-
porting the government? How long before they come for us?*

The only person who kept Adenah from becoming petrified was Big Ma. "Don't worry, 'Denah," her grandmother
would calmly say. "It's going to be all right. I won't let any harm
come to you or anyone else in our family." The words were
comforting to Adenah—and so was Big Ma's air of confidence.
Also reassuring to the girl was that she had yet to see any real
fear in her grandmother's eyes.

The rebels' presence had a chilling effect on business in
Foya. Few vendors or customers showed up at the market during the first couple of weeks. When it was relatively safe to go
outside, Big Ma told Adenah, "Don't look at the rebels in the
eye. Try to make yourself invisible as you go about your business. Don't give them any cause to talk to you."

Three weeks after the NPFL's takeover of the town,
Adenah helped Big Ma reopen the restaurant, setting out tables
and chairs on the front porch. At first, the only customers were
rebels because most people were still too afraid to venture out
for anything other than necessities. As the lone waitress,
Adenah served boiled cassava leaves and potato greens, spicy
soup, and a Liberian staple called fufu (a boiled, doughy starch
rolled into small ovals).

Adenah didn't enjoy waiting on the rebels, but she
remained polite. As long as her grandmother was nearby,
the girl felt safe. *They won't do anything to me*, she thought. *They*

would have to kill Big Ma first. Some of the rebels were polite and paid for their food. Others, though, just walked off without leaving any money.

Rumors started to spread that the rebels no longer viewed Big Ma favorably. They were miffed that she had arranged for Theresa to slip out of town during the night and find a safe haven at a relative's house in Sierra Leone. They were also beginning to suspect that Big Ma had money stashed in the house—money that could help fund their uprising.

Adenah noticed that her grandmother's eyes, which had projected a steely defiance ever since the rebels arrived in town, were showing fear for the first time. Adenah had never seen that look on Big Ma before, and now the girl was scared. At night in bed, Adenah kept thinking terrible thoughts, which made falling asleep difficult: *What will they do to her? What will they do to me?*

One night, she found herself in the grip of what seemed a frightening nightmare. An intruder—no doubt a rebel—had sneaked into her room and clamped his hand firmly over her mouth. She tried to scream, tried to shake him off, but she couldn't do either. Then Adenah woke up—only to realize there really was a hand over her mouth.

Before she could utter a sound, she heard Big Ma whisper in the darkness, "Shush. It's me. Come, come, come, come!"

Her heart pounding, Adenah sat up and asked, "What's going on?"

"Get dressed," Big Ma said. "We're leaving right now."

"Where?"

"Away from here because it's no longer safe. Don't take anything. We must hurry."

Donning a T-shirt under a denim dress, Adenah put on slippers and, while still in a sleepy fog, followed her grandmother and her cousins outside in the dead of night, where other relatives and family friends had gathered.

"We're walking to Koindu," Big Ma explained, referring to a major diamond-mining town that was 10 times larger than Foya. Koindu, where Big Ma's sister and brother-in-law owned a big house, was about 20 miles (32 kilometers) away in Sierra Leone.

"But you can't walk that far," Adenah said, knowing that an auto accident a few years earlier had left the woman with seriously injured knees that never healed properly.

"I hired two men to carry me," Big Ma said, pointing to a wheelbarrow. "Now, let's go. And everyone be quiet. We can't let the rebels know we're sneaking out."

Concerned that using the main road, or any road, raised the risk of rebels spotting them, they took footpaths that snaked through the brush. However, some sections on their route had no paths, so they created their own in the tall grass. Along the way, they met up with other townspeople who also were escaping. Numbering about 25 women and children and a few men, the group remained silent, knowing that any loud noise, any cough or sneeze, might attract the rebels' attention.

By walking slowly and carefully, they avoided any encounters with the rebels. Shortly before dawn, when they were within a few miles of the border, the tire of the wheelbarrow burst. The two men who had been pushing Big Ma no longer could transport her.

"You must go on without me," she told the group. "My farm is close by, and I can stay in the little house there."

"No, we can't leave you behind," protested Adenah, who was beginning to cry.

"Hush," her grandmother said, wiping tears from the girl's cheeks. "I'll be fine." No amount of pleading by Adenah could convince Big Ma to change her mind. "I'll make arrangements to join up with you later in Koindu. You must go."

After the men agreed to help her walk to the farmhouse, the group continued on its way. Adenah wept quietly, fretting over her grandmother's safety. *What if the rebels find her? Will they torture her? Will they kill her? Will anyone be able to save her?*

As the sun came up, they crossed the border into Sierra Leone. They were now refugees, but at least they felt safe. Having escaped from the rebels, the group's mood had brightened considerably, although Adenah still hated leaving her grandmother alone on the farm. The girl and family members reached the home of her great-aunt in Koindu, where they settled in for what they hoped would be a short time before they could return to their quiet lives in Foya.

But that likelihood grew dimmer by the day. Koindu was taking in a growing number of refugees from Liberia as well as receiving disturbing reports of bloodshed throughout the region. So many Liberians were fleeing that a makeshift refugee camp sprang up outside of Koindu, mostly populated with Kissi, like Adenah.

The girl felt lucky she had a roof over her head, food on the table, and family around her. But she was depressed and worried about Big Ma. Every day, Adenah waited for her grandmother to show up. But there was no sign of her and no word that she was okay.

After a week of anguish, Adenah decided to find her grandmother. Waiting until everyone was asleep, the girl tiptoed out of the house and headed for the Liberian border. Wary of rebels, she walked through the brush until she reached the little farmhouse in the wee hours of the morning. The door was locked. She knocked a few times but there was no response. Disheartened and weary, Adenah lay on the front porch and fell asleep.

She was awakened at daybreak by the screams of her grandmother. "'Denah! 'Denah! What are you doing here?"

"I came to see if you were all right."

After they embraced and wept out of relief that both were alive, Big Ma asked, "How did you get here?"

"I walked."

Big Ma threw her hands up. "It's so dangerous around here. You could have been killed by the rebels."

"I was worried about you. You said you were coming but you never came."

Big Ma hugged Adenah and vowed, "You're never going to leave my sight."

Soon, a man arrived with a different wheelbarrow and, with Adenah walking beside him, transported Big Ma safely to her sister's house in Koindu. Adenah could finally relax.

There was no school for Adenah and her younger cousins. The grown-ups tried to make life as normal as possible for the kids by giving them school lessons and time to play— and by shielding them from hearing reports of massacres and torture.

Adenah noticed that the refugees at the camp were lacking the kinds of fresh vegetables and other food that they enjoyed in Liberia. Following the age-old commercial rule "find a need and fill it," Adenah and her cousin Kandor, who was in her twenties, set up their own little business supplying goods to the refugees. It was dangerous work because it meant walking into rebel-occupied territory in Liberia, buying the items, and bringing them back to Koindu to sell at a profit.

The toughest part was convincing their grandmother to let them do it. Realizing the refugees could use the produce, Big Ma relented. Traveling at night, Adenah and Kandor trekked through the countryside and arrived at Foya at daybreak. They bought peppers, potato greens, vegetables, spices, and other items that weren't available to refugees in Koindu. After waiting until nightfall, the pair loaded the produce in baskets, which they carried on their heads for the long walk back to the camp, and showed up there the next morning to sell their goods. For a skinny 12-year-old girl, the task wasn't easy, but it was profitable.

Adenah brought back more than just produce to sell. She also brought news from Foya of more beatings, more torture. The girl also learned that shortly after she and her family had fled the town, the rebels burst into Big Ma's house and ransacked the place, looking for valuables and any money the woman might have hidden. There was no way for anyone to know at the time whether the rebels found the stash that Big Ma had indeed buried before leaving.

During these trips, Adenah and Kandor never had any confrontations with the rebels, partly because the intruders didn't realize the two were Big Ma's nieces. If the rebels had known, the pair risked being seized and held for ransom.

Liberian refugees who fled into Sierra Leone thought they were safe from the mayhem in their native country. But they weren't. The civil war that was wreaking havoc in Liberia was beginning to infect Sierra Leone. Along the border, a new group of radicals known as the Revolutionary United Front (RUF) had joined forces with Charles Taylor's NPFL. In 1991, they attacked Bomaru, a village in Sierra Leone, killing 14 people. Sierra Leone soldiers rushed to Bomaru, which was near Koindu, and drove the rebels out. Believing most villagers had sided with the rebels, the soldiers then brutalized the civilians—and even took their possessions, which the rebels had stolen but left behind during the retreat.

The RUF insurgents, who tried to look scary by painting

their faces and wearing fright wigs, were heartless. If local chiefs didn't cooperate, they were murdered. So were villagers who tried to escape or refused to give up produce and livestock. The RUF also forced civilians to carry stolen sacks of coffee and cocoa to Liberia, which were exchanged for weapons and ammunition.

It was only a matter of time before the rebels reached Koindu.

Returning from another buying trip to Foya, Adenah was greeted by a friend who had stunning news: "Your dad is here, and he's come to take you away."

Throughout most of her childhood, Adenah had little contact with her father, Kingsley Bayoh, or her mother, Gertrude, both unmarried Liberians on work visas in the United States. Big Ma didn't have a phone, so the only communication with them came by way of a few letters with tuition money for the girl's grade school and one or two packages a year. Kingsley was a machinist for a large bakery in New Jersey, and Gertrude was a nurse's assistant.

Adenah didn't know much about America. She had heard stories about its wealth and beauty, its paved roads and fancy cars, its tall buildings and beautiful houses, and food, lots and lots of food. Big Ma, who had visited the US once for a wedding, enjoyed describing the wonders she saw there, especially this fluffy, cold, white stuff called snow. Adenah had developed an ongoing fantasy: living in a sprawling house in America, eating all kinds of food—especially potato salad—and playing in the snow. But she didn't kid herself. The chances of going to the US were slim. And she was okay with that reality because she was living with the one person she loved most in the world—her grandmother.

Now she was staring at her father. Adenah didn't recognize him because she hadn't seen him in years. Kingsley told her he had been worried sick about her safety since the war broke out. He had used his two weeks of vacation time to search for her, and he became frantic because he couldn't find her. When his two weeks were up, he took an unpaid leave of absence to continue scouring the Foya area while dodging rebels.

"What are you doing here?" Adenah asked.

"I've come to take you to America. Wouldn't you like that?"

"But I can't go. I have a business now and I can't leave Big Ma."

Her grandmother shook her head and said, "'Denah, it is best for you to be with your father and mother. You will have a better life—a much safer one—than you will here. This is a wonderful opportunity, and I am so happy for you."

Tears streaming down her cheeks, Adenah blurted, "But I don't want to go without you."

Aware of the rebels' looming threat, Kingsley was becoming impatient. "We have no time to lose," he warned Adenah. "We must leave now."

They faced an uncertain journey of 310 miles (500 kilometers) to Freetown, Sierra Leone's capital city, because the area was teeming with members of the RUF. The plan called for her to stay with relatives in Freetown while Kingsley, upon his return to the US alone, began the lengthy immigration process for her. To Adenah, fleeing again meant giving up her lucrative business, facing an unknown future, and saying good-bye to her cousins and, most importantly, her grandmother.

Big Ma gave Adenah one last warm embrace and said, "When you reach America, continue what you started here because you have everything you need to be successful in life. The next time I see you it will be in the United States. I promise. Oh, and one more thing: Stay away from boys."

Months after arriving safely in Freetown, Adenah immigrated to the United States and attended public high school in Newark, New Jersey. She then put herself through college and graduated from Fairleigh Dickinson University, where she earned a degree in business management. Capitalizing on her penchant for hard work and the lessons she learned from her grandmother, she achieved remarkable success in the business world.

Today, Adenah is the founder and CEO of Adenah Bayoh and Companies, which owns, among other enterprises, IHOP franchises in Paterson and Irvington, New Jersey, and a real-estate development firm with more than 225 million dollars in urban redevelopment projects. In 2015, she was appointed to the prestigious

Federal Reserve Bank of New York's Advisory Council on Small Business and Agriculture. That same year, she was named to Ebony magazine's Power 100 list of influential African Americans.

Adenah credits part of her business success to her life as a refugee. "I came from so much tragedy back home that I can deal with anything that's thrown at me," she says. "I know what it's like to not have very much, so I appreciate everything in America and take nothing for granted. I see a glass as half-full—and I'm grateful that I have a glass.

"Adversity puts you at a crossroads. You can allow it to victimize you or propel you. Escaping the war made me hungry for opportunity. I figured out that there was no problem for which I could not find a solution if I dedicated all of my efforts and smarts to it. So, I bring that tenacity, work ethic, and commitment to everything I do."

Jenneh "Big Ma" Viskinda immigrated to the United States in 1993 and, along with Adenah, became an American citizen in 2002. She died in 2016 at the age of 76, leaving a lasting legacy.

Says Adenah, "My grandmother would always say, 'You have to wake up before everyone else does and do more than everyone else.' I watched my grandmother navigate her way through many challenges. She told me that to be successful, there is just no substitute for hard work. I hope to instill that idea in my two children [son Adekunle Alli Saa Monxhwedy and daughter Jenneh Monxhwedy], just as my grandmother instilled that in me."

Adenah's love for family is matched only by her love for this country. "What makes America really America is that my story wouldn't happen anyplace else but here," she declares. "I'm a woman, I'm a black, and I'm a refugee. It doesn't matter where you are from or whether or not you are a refugee. You are given a chance to achieve the American dream."

THE FIELDS OF MISERY

HANN SOY
Cambodia

From 1975 to 1979, the ruthless communist party known as the Khmer Rouge ruled Cambodia and turned the Southeast Asian country into a nation of murder, mayhem, and misery.

Trying to create a rural, classless society, the Khmer Rouge stripped everybody of their basic rights and banned money, private property, schools, universities, religion, public transportation, and even common entertainment and foreign clothes. They tore children from families and made them slaves or manipulated them into soldiers who carried out orders without question, even if it meant shooting their parents. Family members weren't allowed to show any public emotion—especially affection—to each other without risking punishment.

Pol Pot, the leader of the Khmer Rouge, forced millions of citizens out of their cities and homes to work as slave laborers on farms known as collectives, where they suffered from abuse, disease, malnutrition, and starvation. Whether a grade-schooler or an elderly grandmother, every Cambodian in a collective toiled in daily 12-hour shifts without proper food or rest. Even if they had never done manual labor before, they were required to grow *and harvest more than one ton of rice per acre—or face possible execution.*

The Khmer Rouge tortured and killed hundreds of thousands of people simply for being educated. The barbaric regime set up hundreds of special "killing fields" throughout the country, where it executed people considered a burden or threat to the cause or were members of ethnic or religious minorities. According to Yale University's Cambodia Genocide Program, about 1.7 million Cambodians—roughly 20 percent of the population—were murdered at these sites and buried in mass graves. Officials estimate another 1 million or more people died from starvation or disease.

The eyes of bewildered seven-year-old Hann Soy grew big from confusion and fear. Everywhere he looked, he saw black-capped soldiers in black uniforms and red bandannas methodically torching houses and toppling statues. The soldiers were also ransacking a Buddhist temple.

His short legs were trying to keep up with the rest of the family and hundreds of other frightened residents who were fleeing from his ravaged village outside the city of Battambang, Cambodia. Hann didn't need grown-ups to tell him that they were just as scared as he was. He could see the distress and panic etched in their faces. What he couldn't understand was why any of this terror was happening. He had questions, many questions.

"Why are they so mean to us?" he asked his parents. "Why are they kicking us out? Why are they burning our houses? Why are they making us run away?"

"We have no choice but to do what they tell us to do," his father, Sath, replied, his voice choking with resignation. "If we don't, we will be shot."

The boy's older sister, South, who was holding his hand, told him, "Don't talk. Just keep walking fast, and maybe they won't hurt us."

Hann was born in this village to Sath, a barber, and Ngop, a merchant who resold food in a market. But Hann wasn't raised at home with his three brothers and three sisters. Instead, because of religious beliefs, Buddhist monks reared him in the temple that the soldiers were now destroying.

When Hann was born in 1968, he was a sickly baby. His parents, who were devout Buddhists, believed they had been cursed because the year before, Ngop gave birth to a boy who died in infancy. Afraid that Hann faced the same fate, they gave him to the monks to nurture. His parents and siblings visited him often and sometimes took him out for the day. As a toddler, he wondered why he was living in a temple instead of at home with the rest of the family.

In 1975, when Hann was seven, the Khmer Rouge seized control of Cambodia, throwing everyone's life into turmoil.

Shortly after the takeover, soldiers ordered all citizens to leave their homes immediately and start walking into the country-side. There were no exceptions. Even those who were bedridden or in the hospital were forced out.

The people were told they could bring only one set of clothing and nothing else. The Soys rushed to the temple and picked up Hann before joining thousands of other Cambodians from surrounding villages in a somber march to a destination unknown to them.

Now, as this exodus flowed from the cities and villages, Khmer Rouge soldiers barked at the people, "Go to the farm-land, and follow the river!" Brandishing their weapons, they warned, "Anyone left behind will be killed. You are not allowed to remain in your homes. Move!"

Not knowing where they would end up, the Soys walked during the day and slept by the side of the road at night for several dreadful weeks. They tried to survive by snatching fruit off trees and drinking from streams, some of which were pol-luted with corpses of victims who had been shot or had died from starvation or illness. The sight of a dead body used to shock Hann, but after seeing so many over the weeks, he was no longer rattled by it.

The family arrived in a village in Damban 4, one of dozens of small districts within one of seven larger geographical zones set up by the regime. Before the Soys had a chance to get settled, however, soldiers separated Hann's sisters South and Sang and brothers Savy and Savuth—all four were in their late teens or early twenties—from the rest of the family. With no time to say good-bye, they were spirited away to different dambans.

Khmer Rouge authorities told the Soys and hundreds of other displaced families, "Find your own food and make your own shelter. Don't ever try to run away from Damban 4. If we catch you in another damban, we will kill you."

After building a primitive shelter of bamboo and palm fronds, Hann's parents were forced into hard labor. At gunpoint, the Soys and hundreds of other Cambodians in the damban cleared forests, made trails, built roads, and dug a reservoir. Hann took care of his younger sister, Yath, and younger brother, Ho.

Every waking moment was stressful for Hann because on any given day, soldiers would swoop into the damban, grab children, and drag them off to slave labor camps in other dambans. He always worried he would be next. Like other kids, Hann was required to attend a Khmer Rouge school, where students were being brainwashed into believing that the only way of life was Cambodia's severe form of communism, where most everyone was a peasant who worked in the fields for the good of the country.

What wasn't taught was an open secret: The Khmer Rouge feared educated people and were executing anyone who was considered well read. To prevent being murdered, literate people pretended they were uneducated. Hann's parents didn't need to pretend. They had little schooling, unlike his uncle, who was a pilot for the Cambodian Air Force before the takeover. He was executed.

About a year after the Soys arrived at the village in Damban 4, the Khmer Rouge appeared and began rounding up more children. A soldier pointed to Hann and told his parents, "He's going with us. He's old enough now to take care of himself."

No, no! Hann thought. *I don't want to go!* The eight-year-old yearned to run into the arms of his parents and have them plead his case for remaining with them. But Sath and Ngop couldn't say a word, nor show a trace of emotion, without risking punishment. They still had two younger children to take care of.

As the soldiers led Hann away, the terrified boy stared into the sad eyes of his speechless, heartbroken parents. *This is it*, he thought. *This is the last time I will see them ever again.* Trembling in fear, he burst into tears.

Hann wasn't the only child crying. So were dozens of others who were being loaded into a truck. As the vehicle drove them away, Hann paid attention to the direction it was going and made a point of studying the landmarks it passed. He figured this information would come in handy one day if he had the chance to run away.

The truck motored for hours before dropping the children off at a clump of rice fields. As bad as it was in the village, conditions here were much worse. For starters, there was no shelter. Kids had to sleep on the hard ground under the stars and cover themselves in rice stalks to stay warm on chilly nights.

Every day was the same monotonous, strenuous routine. In the morning, armed soldiers lined up hundreds of children and walked them to the fields. Then, from sunup to sundown, the kids did backbreaking work in the watery rice paddies, cultivating, planting, and then harvesting, which required them to chop and bundle rice stalks. Anyone found slacking was beaten, sometimes fatally.

Around noon, the children were given a brief 30-minute break for their one and only meal of the day—two small scoops of rice in a bowl made from a carved-out coconut shell. The measly food was hardly enough to sustain a growing body or ward off diseases caused by the bacteria, fungi, parasites, and viruses in the water. The barefoot kids fell victim to serious skin ailments, respiratory problems, malaria, tetanus, and hookworm.

To the heartless Khmer Rouge, being sick was no excuse for failing to do your job. The basic rule: If you can't work, you can't live. You'll be shot. Treatable, common illnesses were deadly for many kids because they had no access to medication or health care or even any human compassion. The sick children cried. They collapsed. They died.

One morning, Hann was suffering from a high fever that left his body shaky and drained. He could barely stand. When the boy didn't line up with the others for work, a soldier came over to him and ordered, "Get up and get in line!"

"I'm not feeling well," Hann mumbled.

"If you are too sick to work, there will be no food for you. Why would we waste two spoonfuls of rice on you if you cannot do the job? Why should we bother keeping you alive at all?"

They'll kill me unless I work, Hann reminded himself. Rising unsteadily to his feet, he told the soldier, "I'm one hundred percent okay. I can do the job." The soldier grunted and marched him over to the line of workers. Through sheer willpower, Hann managed to make it through the day.

Starving, thirsty, and exhausted, Hann felt his body weaken. Like the other kids, he begged for more food, water, and rest. But the soldiers ignored the pleas. As the months plodded on, Hann hardly noticed when other rail-thin children, who were just as hungry and fatigued as he was, died on the spot. It was an everyday occurrence in the rice fields, as common as a hawk swooping down and snaring a rodent.

Oh, what I wouldn't give to eat a rat, thought Hann, who had wasted away to 30 pounds. Kids were warned that if they tried to consume any insect, small animal, or even a weed, they would be tied up, beaten, and left to die. But hunger is a powerful force—often stronger than the fear of death itself—and it made children take risky chances. Anytime Hann spotted a cricket, lizard, or snail, he'd glance at the soldiers. If their backs were turned, he'd snatch the insect or critter and eat it alive.

Feeling like the walking dead, he had lost his fear of dying. In fact, there were times when death seemed preferable to this life, if this could even be called a life. But a spirit inside him still flickered with a tiny flame of hope. *I have a one percent chance of living*, he told himself. *At least it's better than zero.*

Through all the sweat and stink and drudgery, Hann clung to one dream—however improbable it seemed—that sustained him from giving up. He dreamed of reuniting with his parents. He missed them terribly and prayed they would still be alive when this nightmare ended or when he escaped to them.

Kids had tried to run off before, slipping away in the middle of the night or disappearing when soldiers weren't looking. A few succeeded; many more failed and paid with their lives. As much as he wanted to escape, Hann never found the right opportunity.

One day, shortly after he had spent a year in the rice fields, he wearily lined up with the other children for their lone daily meal. The perpetually hungry boy was near the back, looking forward to the best part of the day when those two bitty spoonfuls of rice reached his empty stomach. When the boy was next in line, however, the server announced, "The food is gone."

Upset and disbelieving, Hann protested, which immediately brought over a scowling soldier who demanded to know, "What's wrong?"

"They ran out of rice before I had my turn," Hann complained.

"Too bad," the soldier replied coldly. "Get back to work."

Without that meager ration of rice, Hann was famished and desperate. *I have to find something to eat*, he told himself. Scanning the ground as he returned to the rice field, he spotted a live rat. He made a quick circular glance. *Good. The soldiers aren't paying me any attention.* He dropped to the ground and lunged for the rodent. *I got it! I got it!* Quickly jumping to his feet, he stuffed the rat in his pocket.

"What are you doing?" demanded a soldier from behind him.

Startled and scared, Hann wheeled around and faced a surly soldier. "Uh, nothing, sir," the boy replied. "I, um, fell down." *I hope he didn't see what I did.*

"Did you eat during the break?" asked the soldier, now joined by two comrades.

"Oh, yes, sir," Hann lied. "I had plenty to eat. You people give us lots to eat."

"What do you have in your pocket?"

Hann felt the blood drain from his head. *They've caught me. I'm as good as dead.* He gulped and replied, "I have a rat."

"We know why you did it."

"Yes, sir. I'm sorry I lied. I haven't eaten today because they ran out of rice." *Maybe they'll let me eat the rat.*

Wanting the other children to watch, the soldier glowered at Hann and hissed, "So you think you're more special than the others, that it's okay for you to eat what the others can't?"

Before Hann could answer, the soldier hit him in the head with the butt of his rifle. The other two slugged him until he fell to the ground. Then they took turns kicking him, beating him, and clubbing him over the head with the rifle.

Before the final blow knocked him out cold, Hann thought, *I'm going to die.*

Later that night, the boy regained consciousness. His eye hurt and was swollen shut. When he touched his head, he felt blood all over his face. He was in such pain, especially in one leg, that he could barely move. *I wonder if my leg is broken.*

Bruised and battered, he tried several times before he could stand up. He looked around and, in the moonlight, saw that the soldiers had tossed him in a roadside ditch of bamboo. *They probably think they beat me to death.*

Hann realized that when they had thrown him in the ditch, he landed on an upright jagged piece of bamboo, which tore a gash in his leg. Weak and in terrible pain, he passed out again. When he woke up, Hann thought, *Why should I stay here? They think I'm dead. If they find me, they'll just try to kill me. I should take off. Other kids have run away.* Or at least tried. He couldn't count the number of children who were caught and executed on the spot. But at this point, he had nothing to lose but his life. *Maybe getting beat up this badly is a good thing. It's given me the chance to escape.*

He limped to a nearby river, where he washed his wound and the blood off his face. Then he guzzled water. Just quenching his thirst seemed to energize him. Despite the jabbing pains in his leg, head, and torso, he felt a surge of hope as he left behind the appalling rice fields.

Hann knew the general direction of the village where he

last saw his parents. It was at the base of a mountain that loomed in the distance, lit by the moon. *Keep walking toward the mountain*, he repeatedly told himself.

With a bum leg and a closed eye, he lurched through the jungle until the sun came up. Then he hid in a bamboo thicket and passed out again. When he regained consciousness, he continued his trek, slowly, one painful step after another. Hann avoided roads and well-worn paths because he knew the Khmer Rouge were close by. He heard their trucks and their voices as they rumbled past. Working his way along a riverbank, he saw dozens of corpses floating downstream.

I have to make it back to my village. I don't want to die in the jungle. I need to see my family again. But are they alive? Are they still in the same village?

With each passing hour, the hope of being with his family glowed a little bit brighter. So did his mood because he was eating something other than a dollop of rice. He was plucking fruit off the trees and pulling potatoes out of the ground.

After three arduous days, Hann entered the village, where about 1,000 slave laborers were just trying to survive. A family friend came up to him and, looking surprised, said, "Hann, what are you doing here?"

"I escaped," Hann said. "I came to see my parents. Please tell me, are they alive?" His body tensed up as he waited for the answer.

"Yes," the man replied, uttering the one word that Hann most wanted to hear. "The last time I saw them they were living in the same spot they were when you were taken away. But, Hann, they're not the same."

Not the same? What does he mean by that?

"You better go now, but be extra careful. The Khmer Rouge are constantly patrolling this area, looking for people who escaped."

His heart beating in anticipation of seeing his parents again, Hann limped toward the family's shelter that had been their home for nearly two years. From a short distance away, he spotted a man and a woman sitting under a tree. *They look like Mom and Dad, but they seem too skinny and too old to be them.* He moved in closer. *It is them!*

His father, Sath, looked up at the scrawny nine-year-old who was approaching them. Tears rolled down Sath's drawn cheeks. In a quivering voice, he said, "My son? Is that really you?"

"Yes, Dad. It's me."

Then Ngop let out a yelp of joyous surprise, alerting Hann's two younger siblings, Yath and Ho, who joined in the reunion. Their emotions were too strong to hold back. They hugged, wept, and hugged some more. Missing from the gathering were his four oldest siblings, whose whereabouts and fates were unknown by the family.

His parents bombarded him with questions: Where were you? How did you survive? Why did you escape? How did you get here?

He told them about the misery he had endured in the rice fields, adding, "I saw death around me every day."

Sath gave an understanding nod and said, "That's the way it is for everyone."

"I can't believe you escaped," Ngop said.

"They thought they killed me, and that gave me my chance," Hann said. "I just had to see you again."

While sharing stories of their forced labor, Hann couldn't get over how much his parents had changed. They had aged and had lost weight, down to about 60 pounds each. He noticed how weak and frail they were, forgetting that he, too, was weak and frail.

"What are the chances of surviving in this village?" Hann asked his father.

"For the next few days, probably pretty good," Sath replied. "But for any length of time, it's zero. Staying in the village is just another way of waiting to be executed."

"I heard from older kids in the rice fields that people are escaping through the jungle, trying to make it to Thailand," said Hann, referring to the neighboring country to the west, which was not communist. "If we make it there, we will be safe."

"But if we are caught, we will be executed," Sath countered.

"We have to take that risk, Dad. Why stay here? We'll die in this village. At least if we try to escape, we have a chance—a small one—of getting out of Cambodia and away from the Khmer Rouge."

Hann continued to prod his parents until they agreed to escape. Waiting for nightfall, the family sneaked out of the village, knowing there was no going back. They eventually met up with his older sister Sang, who joined them in a journey that was much more strenuous and challenging than they ever imagined. Over the next two years, they snaked through the dense jungle, where dangerous animals and treacherous soldiers searched for prey. Every step required extra care because the Khmer Rouge had planted deadly landmines everywhere.

The Soys camped out in makeshift shelters, hid in caves, and often stayed for weeks at a time in other villages. Suffering from chronic malnutrition, and often hunger and thirst, they ate leaves, fruit, roots, and occasionally a small animal they had caught. Whenever they saw a creek or a pond, they thought they had won the lottery. When it rained, they grabbed giant palm fronds and collected the water. Sometimes they fell ill from consuming the wrong plant or tainted water. Other times, they dealt with insect bites and scratches that became infected.

Just survive one day at a time, Hann told himself. In such a harsh environment, it was hard to think of the future other than trying to get through the next minute, the next hour. But the ultimate goal of reaching a refugee camp in Thailand was always front and center in his mind.

The Soys walked mostly at night—Hann was barefoot—and concealed themselves in the brush whenever soldiers approached. Often, they encountered families from other dambans who were also trying to reach Thailand. The Soys and their fellow escapees shared food and any information about the Khmer Rouge. That's how the family learned soldiers were hiding near watering holes, waiting to kill thirsty escapees and planting landmines around the perimeter. The small explosions the Soys heard usually meant that an unfortunate soul had tripped a landmine.

In 1979, during their second year on the run, the family found out that Vietnamese military forces had invaded Cambodia and were fighting the Khmer Rouge. The war crept close to the Soys, and they began hearing the sounds of mortar rounds, machine guns, and firefights. If the skirmishes were in front of them, they sheltered in place or stayed in a village so they wouldn't be caught in the crossfire. Whenever the battles moved elsewhere, the family would head for the next village.

By the end of the year, the Soys finally crossed into Thailand and settled in the Khao-I-Dang (also known as KID) refugee camp. The huge compound of bamboo and thatch houses became the haven for tens of thousands of Cambodian refugees, who were arriving at the rate of 1,600 a day. The camp was just a few miles from the Cambodian border, but to refugees like Hann it felt like a million miles away from the horrors of the Khmer Rouge. For the first time since the regime seized power, Hann felt safe.

"We ran away from hell," he told his family. "We had a one percent chance of surviving, and we made it. We deserve a new life. I want a new life." He hoped to start over in a "third country"—a term refugees use referring to the nation that accepts them as immigrants with the possibility of citizenship.

(The first country is the one refugees fled from, and the second country is the temporary one where they fled to.)

Hann promised himself that he would become a better person if a country would give him the opportunity to reach his full potential. When he looked into his future, though, several unknowns blurred his vision: *How long would he remain a refugee? Would any country accept him? Where would he go next? How would he adapt to a new culture and language?*

When the refugee camp became overcrowded, Western countries tried to relieve the pressure by setting up a vetting system to move refugees permanently to other countries. This method included an interview. Those who passed could begin the lengthy immigration process.

Every day, Hann went to the camp office to see whose names were posted for an interview. One morning, he saw his father's name—representing the family—on a list for possible immigration to Belgium. Sath did the interview with Belgian officials, but it turned into a disaster. He was still so trauma-tized from years of abuse by the Khmer Rouge that he couldn't answer simple questions or give the birthdates of his children. Authorities thought he wasn't honest and forthcoming, so they rejected him and his family for immigration.

The Soys waited in camp for another year before given a second chance, this time with American officials. Hann didn't know much about the United States other than it was a country brimming with great opportunities, which he wanted.

The family felt the pressure, knowing it might have run out of options. Before the interview, Hann told his father, "Dad, this time you must do what it takes to get us out of here and get us to where we should be—the United States. We all risked our lives to flee Cambodia. We've suffered enough. It's time to leave the refugee camp for a better life."

Extremely nervous because of what was at stake, the family joined Sath for the interview. With Hann by his side, Sath answered all questions clearly and firmly. He also told the officials, "Everyone in my family has been through a lot. My three oldest children are likely dead. I have a scar from what the Khmer Rouge did to me. My son Hann has a scar from a severe beating to prove what he's been through. We're not here at KID by choice or even want to stay. We ran for our lives and are here to survive, to have food, shelter, and be free of violence. Starting a new life in America means everything to us. If you allow us to come to the US and if you provide my children with an education so they will become good citizens, I am willing to work for your country for free."

Hann was proud of his father, but wondered if the interview went well enough to pass the first hurdle of immigration. He anxiously studied the body language of the officials as they paced back and forth and talked in English—a language he didn't understand—about the Soys. Judging from the stern looks on their faces, he didn't think the verdict would be favorable.

Hann held his breath as the main official walked over to the family. With the help of a translator, he shook Sath's hand and said, "Congratulations, sir. You and your family are going to the United States."

The immigration process took a frustratingly long time before 15-year-old Hann, his parents, sister Yath, and brother Ho arrived in Boston in 1983. His sister Sang Say, who got married at Khao-I-Dang, and her husband, Horn Tong, joined them later. Having difficulty adjusting to American life and struggling with the language, the entire family moved in 1987 to Stockton, California, which had a thriving community of Cambodian immigrants. There, the Soys flourished.

In 1990, the family learned that Han's sister South had died of illness during the Khmer Rouge reign of terror. His older brothers Savy and Savuth had worked as slave laborers building roads in another damban and tried but failed to escape. Savy lost a leg when he stepped on a landmine. He and Savuth remain in Cambodia with their families. Sang and Ho, who live in Stockton, and Yath, who resides in Long Beach, California, are American citizens with families of their own. Sath and Ngop died in 1995 and 2012 respectively.

Hann, who became an American citizen in 2011, and his wife, Kosal Kruth, who was born in the KID camp, live in Stockton and have three children, Julie, Sallida, and Rachhaya. Now a child welfare advisor, Hann has been working for the Lodi (California) Unified School District since 1990. He spends much of his time speaking in schools, using his life story to help motivate troubled young people. "I tell kids that the emotional wound from those days in Cambodia will stay with me forever, but life goes on and I continue to grab at opportunities," he says. "My life story shows you can still be whatever you want to be no matter how difficult it seems. Over the years, I've received thousands of letters from people who thanked me for inspiring them not to give up on themselves when their lives turned bad."

In 2016, Hann and Kosal returned to Cambodia to lay his parents' cremains in their final resting place in a Buddhist temple. "I went back to see my village," he says. "It had been demolished, and our house was no longer there. But a part of me will always be there."

THE SIEGE OF SREBRENICA

ELVIR AHMETOVIĆ
Bosnia

After World War II, the Eastern European country of Yugoslavia was made up of six republics—Bosnia (officially known today as Bosnia and Herzegovina), Serbia, Montenegro, Croatia, Slovenia, and Macedonia. Various ethnic groups, including Orthodox Christian Serbs, Muslim Bosniaks, Catholic Croats, and Muslim ethnic Albanians, tended to live in specific regions.

For more than four decades, the republics were relatively tolerant of each other's ethnic differences. But in 1991, Yugoslavia spiraled out of control when the republics began seeking their own independence. Exploiting the split-up and stoking ethnic hatred, Serbian president Slobodan Milošević convinced Serbs that Muslims and other ethnic groups posed a threat to Serbian rights. The Serbs then launched a murderous campaign of "ethnic cleansing"—the systematic removal and killing of an unwanted ethnic group—in a merciless quest to create a "greater Serbia."

The first republic to spill blood was Croatia. Claiming to protect Serbs, the Yugoslav People's Army and Serbian militia forces invaded

Croatia, carrying out mass executions of Croat civilians, burying them in mass graves, and driving 170,000 people from their homes.

After Bosnia declared its independence in April 1992, Serbian forces started an ethnic cleansing of Muslim Bosniaks in the republic through brutal human-rights abuses. In a war that lasted nearly four years, more than 100,000 civilians were killed and more than two million displaced. The most horrific week occurred in July 1995, when more than 8,300 Bosniak men and boys were slaughtered in what became known as the Srebrenica genocide—the worst massacre in Europe since the Holocaust.

Fourteen-year-old Elvir Ahmetović hunkered down with the rest of his family in a dank, musty cellar, enduring the latest bombardment unleashed by Bosnian Serbs. With every thunderous blast, he could feel the dirt floor vibrate and the rock walls shudder.

The cellar made a good bomb shelter, which is why, at the impact from the first salvo, people from the nearest houses dropped what they were doing and rushed into the cramped underground chamber to wait out the barrage with the Ahmetovićs. Sometimes the shelling lasted for only an hour, sometimes for most of the day.

Having gone through so many of these attacks—it seemed as if they were almost a daily occurrence—Elvir accepted them as just the way it was during war. This submission to reality didn't make him any less scared; in fact, there were times when he was petrified. But there was nothing he could do except what he was doing now—staying crouched in a cellar and hoping a shell didn't make a direct hit.

Elvir could tell by the sound of the blasts if they had come from a mortar round, artillery shell, grenade, or tank. He could also sense how far away they were. The close explosions shook the shelter hard enough to cause dust from the ceiling to rain down on everyone. What he didn't want to hear, but too often did, were the screams and shouts of anguish from somewhere out there of the injured or dying or of their grieving loved ones.

It had been three years—going on four—since he and his family had fled their home and had holed up in this tiny cellar. Home. He wondered if it was still there.

Before the war, Elvir was a happy kid enjoying a simple life in a serene Bosnian village near the town of Srebrenica. His father, Bajro, worked in a nearby mine, while his mother, Zibija, stayed at home and took care of the family, which included Elvir's younger sister, Mirela. Doing some blacksmith work on the side, Bajro made enough to own a modest house and land to grow a little garden and raise chickens, goats, and a cow.

Throughout the region, each community's inhabitants came from separate ethnic groups. Elvir's were Muslim Bosniaks, while Orthodox Christians populated the neighboring village. The differences in religion or ethnicity didn't mean much to Elvir or his classmates at school, which served a mix of Muslim and Christian students from the area's small communities. Other than the different way they spelled their names and the religious holidays they celebrated, the kids assumed they were all the same.

In their free time, they relished unsupervised outdoor fun together. The forest acted as their playground, the perfect venue to engage in games of war with guns fashioned out of sticks and pieces of wood. When they weren't playing marbles, they were kicking soccer balls on any unused patch of grass they could find. Elvir didn't view his pals as Muslim or Christian or Serb or Bosniak; they were simply friends.

But by 1991, when Elvir was 10 years old, he was aware of the national tension simmering between Serbs and Bosniaks because that friction filtered into his school. Students from different ethnic groups began bickering over trivial matters and dropping friendships with those who weren't just like them. Talk of war in Bosnia intensified.

A Serb acquaintance asked Bajro if he was looking forward to the conflict between Serbs and Bosniaks. "I don't believe it will happen in Bosnia," Bajro replied. "We are civilized people, after all. Surely we won't let the situation escalate so badly that it breaks out into war."

"Well, I'm looking forward to it, and I will participate in it," the man declared. "War is coming."

In May 1992, Bosnian Serb forces, with the backing of

Serbian president Slobodan Milošević and the Serb-dominated Yugoslav army, began bombarding Bosnia's capital, Sarajevo. Days later, Serb paramilitary forces in armored vehicles, tanks, and trucks rumbled into Elvir's unprotected village. After ordering everyone to assemble, the Serbs demanded the villagers surrender all their weapons. No one had any guns other than a few elderly men, who gave up their hunting rifles. For an unknown reason, the Serbs seized two of Elvir's cousins and spirited them away. His cousins were never seen again.

Before leaving the village, the Serbs announced they would return the next day. That night, many inhabitants abandoned their homes out of fear over what the Serbs might do. Elvir, his four-year-old sister, Mirela, and his parents gathered blankets and personal belongings and hid in the woods with their neighbors for several days.

As an 11-year-old, Elvir couldn't understand why the grown-ups were so afraid. He and his friends thought the soldiers, machine guns, tanks, and campouts made for an exciting adventure.

But over the next week, he heard unsettling accounts from victims and witnesses of Serbian brutality, like what happened to Bego Buhić, Elvir's beloved neighbor. He was like a family member, who often came over to the Ahmetovićs' home to share a drink with Bajro and play cards. When the Serbs showed up, Bego chose to stay rather than run and hide. Shortly after the Serbs occupied the village, Bego's body was found sprawled in the grass.

Troubling reports from around the region stunned the local Bosniaks: Serb snipers were picking off civilians as they tried to secure food and water. Serb militiamen were executing men, torturing teenagers, and attacking women. Serb officials were breaking into Bosniaks' houses, looting them, and, in some cases, occupying them.

Bosniaks assumed the Yugoslav army would end the conflict so they could return to their homes in a week or so. However, the military was under the control of the Serbs, so it would not be helping the Bosniaks—quite the opposite.

In the woods, elders talked with the villagers about what to do next. Some wanted to head back home and surrender; others chose to move deeper into the forest. The Ahmetovićs broke camp and hiked farther away to a remote village in a region that was still under the control of the Bosnian army. Elvir prepared himself for the new certainty of war—returning home was not days away. No, it was more like months, maybe even years away. Or never.

When the homeless, destitute family reached the village of Gabelje, they sought out an acquaintance who offered them the most basic of shelters—a dank, dark cellar where he kept potatoes and grains. Built out of stone and accessed from the outside, the underground chamber had no windows, no electricity, no heat, no running water, and no furniture. It had a dirt floor—and rats, lots of rats, some as big as shoes. Crawling up walls and scurrying along the ceiling rafters, the rats were like annoying household pets that Elvir learned to ignore.

For beds, the family lay boards on the floor in the corner and put a few blankets on top to serve as a mattress. Elvir and the others worked in the owner's fields, harvesting corn, oats, and wheat for him in exchange for a portion of the grains. The boy herded sheep and goats out to pasture, while Bajro made and repaired tools. To supplement their meager diet, the family picked plums, apples, and pears.

The Ahmetovićs took their grain to an old water mill, which ground it into a rough flour. Zibija made bread out of the ground oats because it kept their bellies full longer than cornmeal did. The flour from oats still contained the chaff—the husk surrounding the seed—which made the bread scratchy on the throat. Elvir couldn't stand to eat it, so his mother saved the cornmeal for him. She cooked on a wood-burning stove, which was used to heat water drawn from a stream.

The village was tucked behind a hill, so the civilians were safe from Serbian tanks. However, the Serbs regularly shelled the area with artillery and mortar rounds. The cellar became the safest place for the Ahmetovićs and neighbors to be during attacks.

One hot August day in 1992, about a dozen people began gathering hay in a field that was well within firing range of Serb militiamen who had taken up positions nearby. Normally, the villagers worked the fields at night in the moonlight because the Serbs didn't usually shell the area after dark.

But this day seemed different. It was peaceful and free from any shelling. In fact, there was talk—not confirmed by anyone in authority—that a temporary ceasefire was in place. Zibija thought this would be a good time for her and Mirela to help collect hay, so they joined the workers. Elvir remained in the cellar while Bajro stayed to work in his makeshift blacksmith shop, where he was sharpening people's axes and agricultural tools and making horseshoes.

The field lay fully exposed with no hill to protect anyone if a tank fired on them. But the workers assumed they weren't in danger. There was a ceasefire, right?

If there was, it was broken. The blast from a Serbian tank rocked the tranquil day. The shell landed about 100 yards from the workers, exploding in a geyser of dirt, hay, and shrapnel. Screaming, panic-stricken workers sprinted toward the woods.

The tank fired another round. This one exploded in a cluster of women and spewed jagged, red-hot shrapnel in all directions. Fragments sliced into the shoulder of a woman and into the back of another, fatally wounding them; a metal shard instantly killed a child; and a razor-sharp piece hit a woman's stomach.

Elvir could tell by the sound that the Serbs had fired on the field where his mother and sister were gathering hay. He bolted from the cellar and raced toward the field. On his mad dash, he heard people shrieking and crying that a shell had struck several workers.

Then he heard someone yell in sorrow, "Mirela is dead!"

The unfathomable news shocked Elvir to his core, and he felt himself lose control. He dropped to the ground and wailed, burying his tear-drenched face in the dirt. *No, this can't be true!*

It just can't! Sobbing so hard he could hardly breathe, he finally gathered himself. He got up and ran into the field, where he saw his mother staggering toward him. She was holding her stomach, which shrapnel had torn open.

"Mirela is dead!" she cried out. "And I've been hit!"

Reeling from the devastation of losing his sister and the anguish of seeing his mother suffering from a life-threatening wound, Elvir felt like collapsing again, but found the strength to stay on his feet. He rushed over to Zibija, who was doubled over in pain, and helped her from the field.

"I won't make it," she moaned, wincing in agony. "My abdomen is cut open."

"We'll get you help," Elvir said.

"It's too late for that. Besides, there are no hospitals around here. Elvir, when I die, I want you to stay with your father."

"Don't talk like that. I can't lose you, too."

Showing incredible grit, Zibija lurched her way for another half mile before she finally collapsed. Villagers picked her up and carried her to a truck—one of only a few in the whole area—which transported her to Srebrenica, about 12 miles (20 kilometers) away. She was brought to a makeshift urgent-care facility staffed by well-meaning people who had limited medical skills. Because they had no medicine or antibiotics, there wasn't much they could do but watch victims die from ordinary wounds that became infected.

After Bajro saw how badly Zibija was hurt, he was too upset to console Elvir. The only words that came out of his mouth were uncomfortably blunt: "Your mother won't make it. No one thinks she has a chance, so prepare yourself and don't hold out hope for any miracles."

Elvir didn't know sadness could hurt so much. The loss of his sister—and likely his mother—was simply too excruciating to accept, the tragedy too impossible to comprehend. He kept weeping. He was too crippled emotionally to attend Mirela's funeral, which took place the next day. She was buried in a local cemetery in a ceremony attended by Bajro and grieving villagers and refugees.

A few days later, Elvir learned that his mother was still alive. In a great stroke of luck, a visiting surgeon from the city of Tuzla had sneaked past the Serbs and was volunteering at the temporary medical center when Zibija was brought in. He performed an emergency operation and patched her up. Amazingly, she made it through the critical first few days without a serious infection and eventually returned to the family's underground home.

As relieved as he was to have his mother back, Elvir agonized over Mirela's death. Every night, he would see her in his dreams, happy and innocent and full of life. Every morning, he would wake up and know that Mirela was gone, and he would relive her death all over again.

His parents wouldn't, or couldn't, talk to Elvir about the tragedy. The only way they could cope with her loss was to avoid the subject. Whatever grief they suffered, they hid it from him; he was tormented enough. Zibija, who had a cheery and optimistic personality, did her best to radiate a positive attitude that she hoped would rub off on Elvir.

Shortly after Mirela's death, Elvir's grandparents Husein and Šehrija Jašarević and their sons Nezir, 18, and Nedim, 20, came to live with him and his parents because Serbs had seized their village. The two young men were soon drafted into the Bosnian army and sent to the front line to defend the territory. Months later, the family received news that an enemy grenade had killed Nezir. Once again, the family was plunged into grief.

When winter set in, food became scarce, and the Ahmetovićs were desperate to stave off hunger. Compassionate villagers, who had saved up grains for the winter, shared what little they had to save the refugee family from starvation during those bleak days.

Elvir missed school and his friends. For a few months, on days when it was safe, he attended an improvised school run by volunteers who were the village's most literate people. School supplies were minimal. Whenever Elvir filled his notebook with his class notes, he would erase those he no longer needed so he could reuse the pages.

When spring 1994 arrived, Elvir and his parents had marked two years since fleeing their house. Although life was hard and uncertain, they felt fortunate they had a shelter. Sure, it was a damp, stuffy cellar. But it was home—one made much brighter with the birth of Elvir's sister Alma. They were once again a family of four.

Their joy was muted, however, by the ongoing war. The

besieged Bosnian army was still struggling to hold off attacking Serb forces, which had surrounded nearby Srebrenica and five other towns. The United Nations Security Council finally stepped in. It declared that Srebrenica and a 30-square-mile (78-square-kilometer) area around the town—inhabited by the Ahmetovićs and 60,000 other Bosniaks—was a UN Safe Area and brought in several hundred Dutch soldiers to act as peacekeepers.

As part of the deal, the UN stripped Bosniak defenders of their heavy weapons and set up UN checkpoints around the territory. But this effort didn't end hostilities. Bosniaks from inside the territory began carrying out raids on surrounding Bosnian Serb villages after the Serbs regularly blocked the food convoys and UN troop rotations.

The peacekeepers didn't have the manpower or the weapons to hold back the Serbs. And so the war continued. The Ahmetovićs hunkered down in their cellar just trying, like tens of thousands of other Bosniaks, to stay alive as the deadly conflict entered its fourth year.

By now, Muslim villages in central Bosnia had been ethnically cleansed and burnt to the ground. Serbian forces had set up concentration camps, where people were beaten and starved to death. Sarajevo, the country's largest city, was still under siege after three years of bombardment. Serb leader Radovan Karadžić—known as The Butcher of Bosnia—boasted, "Sarajevo will be a black cauldron where Muslims will die. They will disappear . . . from the face of the Earth."

Elvir was living in an insane world where the most harmless activities could get him killed. Several Bosniak children were killed by a Serb mortar round while they were building a snowman. A young boy was blinded by an incoming artillery shell while playing soccer. A little girl died from a sniper bullet while picking flowers for her father.

On July 6, 1995, Serbian forces began an intensive shelling of Srebrenica. They quickly overwhelmed the Dutch soldiers—some of whom were taken hostage—and seized the so-called "safe area," which was no longer safe.

Five days later, Bosnian Serb general Ratko Mladić entered Srebrenica and claimed the town for the Bosnian Serbs. Knowing that the Serbs would target Bosniak males, Bajro, his brother Osman, and Zibija's brother Nedim decided to flee. Osman's 15-year-old son, Munib, chose to go with them. Elvir, now 14, didn't join them because his parents thought he had a better chance of surviving if he stayed behind.

Around midnight, Elvir's father, two uncles, and cousin linked up with a column of 15,000 men and teenage boys that was forming in the nearby mountains for a perilous 63-mile (101-kilometer) journey. They were hoping to reach the safety of the Muslim city of Tuzla, which was protected by the Bosnian army. As the Bosniaks moved out, Serbian military forces began shooting them. Unarmed and without shelter, hundreds of men and boys in the back of the column were mowed down. The rest sprinted into the woods for cover.

The next day, Elvir, his mother, baby sister, grandparents,

and more than 23,000 other refugees hurried toward the main Dutch base at Potočari, 3 miles (5 kilometers) away, seeking a safe haven.

Dutch F-16 fighter planes dropped two bombs on Serb positions, but halted further air strikes after the Serbs threatened to execute the Dutch hostages and bombard refugees with mortar rounds. The Serbs then easily captured the base and kicked out the refugees, who then huddled in neighboring factories or camped out in the woods.

The following day, Mladić strode through Srebrenica, handing out treats and assuring refugees, "No matter if you're old or young, you'll get transport to Tuzla. Don't be afraid— women and children first." The Serb soldiers then began separating all males ages 12 to 77 from the crowd.

The operation to transport women, children, the sick, and elderly to Tuzla by a caravan of trucks and buses got underway only after the United Nations agreed to the Serb demand to pay for the fuel of all the vehicles. While waiting in the throng for hours, Elvir and his family began hearing terrifying accounts of boys being pulled away and killed right in front of their mothers' eyes and of elderly men being hustled away and executed.

Elvir's grandfather Husein was petrified. Elvir and his family were pushing their way through the crowd toward the transports when Husein stopped and told them, "I'll come along in a few minutes. You go ahead." After a few hours, they neared one of the trucks. Husein was nowhere in sight. "Let's go back and look for him," Zibija suggested. But Elvir's grandmother Šehrija said, "No, let's get on the truck. Maybe he'll get on another transport and we'll meet up later."

Suddenly, a Serb soldier eyed Elvir, who was tall for his age, and ordered him to step out of the crowd. Zibija gasped in dismay, believing Elvir would be taken away for good. She grabbed Elvir's arm, but he smiled and said, "I'll be all right."

The soldier ordered him, "Get on the truck and help the women get into the back with their bags and their children."

Elvir jumped onto the transport and assisted the refugees, including his mother, sister, and grandmother. When the truck was full, Elvir whispered to Zibija, "I don't know what to do. Do I get off or stay?"

Zibija replied firmly, "Get down on the floor and be quiet."

Elvir did what he was told. Trucks and buses drove off with the refugees and took them to within 3 miles (5 kilometers) of Tuzla before dropping them off. The Serbs made them hike the rest of the way. As Elvir began walking with his family, he felt a strange mix of emotions. He was relieved that he was so close to a safe zone. But he was also worried. *What if this is some kind of trick, and we're about to be executed?*

It wasn't a trick. The exhausted, hungry, thirsty refugees were greeted by townspeople who handed out food, clothes, and water. The next day, the United Nations transported the refugees to a military base in Tuzla, where thousands of tents covered a huge field.

Every morning in the tent city, Elvir woke up hoping that

his father would arrive. Every night, the boy went to bed disappointed. Soon, men and boys who had been fleeing in the column from the Srebrenica area began trickling into the camp. Weary from their dangerous escape through the mountains, they gave chilling accounts of mayhem and murder.

Survivors said Serb soldiers spread out in the woods, hunting down the Bosniaks like animals, slaughtering thousands and tossing them into mass graves. Those men toward the back of the column were killed by artillery.

Using stolen United Nations equipment and Dutch uniforms taken from the captive Dutch peacekeepers, Serb soldiers used loudspeakers to assure hiding Bosniaks they wouldn't be hurt if they came out of the woods. Tricked into believing the soldiers were Dutch peacekeepers, hundreds surrendered and were last seen at a soccer field on their knees with their hands behind their heads.

Reports surfaced that the day after Elvir arrived in Tuzla, 400 men and boys were yanked out of the transport lines in Srebrenica and murdered. Every day fatigued survivors arrived at the refugee camp, telling more horror stories. There was still no sign of Elvir's father, uncles, cousin, or grandfather. Not knowing if they were dead or alive gnawed at Elvir every hour. He chose not to believe the worst, although with each passing day, the hope he held in his heart for their safe passage was dwindling.

About two weeks after arriving in Tuzla, Elvir was sitting in front of his tent, watching the emotional reunion of a teenage boy with his family. Then Elvir's eyes locked onto a man who was about 20 yards away. The man looked familiar but also seemed different because of his gaunt face, scraggly hair, and withered body. As the man came closer, however, there was no mistaking who he was.

"Mom! Mom!" Elvir shouted into the tent. "It's Dad! He's here!"

Shrieking with joy, Zibija charged out of the tent and dashed into Bajro's arms. As Elvir hugged him too, all three wept with relief.

Elvir's uncles Nedim and Osman eventually showed up. But Osman was upset because he didn't know what had happened to his son Munib. The two lost sight of each other and failed to reunite after their small group became disoriented in the woods. (Months later, they would learn that Munib had been killed.)

During this horrendous week in Srebrenica and the surrounding area, the Serbs had carried out the systematic massacre of 8,372 men and boys—the largest civilian slaughter on European soil since the Holocaust. When reports of this heinous crime reached the international community, Serb forces tried to conceal the crimes by digging up the mass graves of their victims and moving the bodies to other locations.

Elvir's grandfather Husein never showed up at the refugee camp. He likely had been killed in Srebrenica. *Had he stayed with us*, Elvir thought, *he would have been on the truck and survived.*

Living in the refugee camp gave Elvir a feeling of security. For the first time since fleeing his home, he didn't fear for his life. Even so, he couldn't give much thought to his future, not with the bloody conflict still raging in his shattered country.

In December 1995 came the announcement that everyone was waiting for: The war was over. Elvir didn't know what to think or how to feel. He had waited for this moment for such a long time that when it finally arrived, his reaction wasn't anything he expected. He didn't jump up and down in jubilation. Instead, he felt somewhat empty. Peace had come years too late. It had come too late for the thousands of innocent children who perished, like Mirela; too late for the countless victims of brutal torture; too late for the shattered families, like the Ahmetovićs, who were left homeless and heartbroken.

Elvir noticed that most everyone around him reacted like he did. There were no wild celebrations, no big parties, no boisterous cheering. The news was met with a collective indifference because so many families had suffered so much. Whatever joy Elvir and the others felt came from one simple but compelling fact: They had survived.

The Ahmetovićs remained in the Tuzla refugee camp for another year before moving to the devastated city of Sarajevo and into a house that a Serbian owner had abandoned after the war. Elvir,

who hadn't been to a real school since fourth grade, enrolled in seventh grade and, by studying hard, caught up with his classmates. The family barely survived because they were living off Husein's 200-dollar-a-month pension and what Bajro earned making and fixing tools. After living in the house for six years, the family was forced to leave when the real owner sold it to someone else.

Believing there was no reason to remain in Bosnia and Herzegovina, the Ahmetovićs applied for war-refugee status, which the United States granted. In 2002, they arrived in St. Louis, now home to an estimated 70,000 Bosnian immigrants. Elvir earned a bachelor's degree in history from St. Louis University and a master's degree in history from King's College in London, England. He taught in elementary school for two years in St. Louis before accepting a position at the Brentwood (Missouri) School District, where, as an interventionist, he works to improve the grades of students who are slipping behind academically. His parents, grandmother, and sister, Alma, live in St. Louis.

Elvir, who became an American citizen in 2010, says the vast majority of refugees who immigrate to the United States thrive here. "Just the fact that they live in a country where they are safe and don't have to fear for their lives allows them to achieve economic stability," he says. "America would not be the great country it is without immigrants. They are a blessing for the United States because they bring fresh blood that invigorates our culture and economy in so many ways."

For those who were born in the United States, he says, "You need to cherish every moment of freedom in this country. Don't take it for granted because America gives you the opportunity to live life to the fullest. Appreciate all the blessings you have here."

The United Nations Security Council established the International Criminal Tribunal for the former Yugoslavia (ICTY) in The Hague, Netherlands, to prosecute war criminals from the Bosnian War.

Former Serbian president Slobodan Milošević was charged with 66 counts of war crimes, crimes against humanity, and genocide. In 2006, he was found dead in his cell in The Hague, months before his trial was scheduled to end.

In 2016, the ICTY convicted former Bosnian Serb leader Radovan Karadžić of genocide and nine other charges and sentenced him to 40 years in prison for orchestrating Serb atrocities throughout the war. The judge said Karadžić and his military commander, General Ratko Mladić, intended "that every able-bodied Bosnian Muslim male from Srebrenica be killed."

Mladić was charged with war crimes, crimes against humanity, and genocide, but his trial, which began in 2011, had been suspended several times.

By the end of 2016, the court had indicted 161 suspects. Of them, 80 were convicted and sentenced, 18 were acquitted, 13 were sent back to local courts, and 36 had their indictments withdrawn or died.

THE DESPERATE TREK

YUSSUF YUSSUF
Somalia

In 1991, violence erupted in the East African country of Somalia after militias ousted dictator Siyad Barre and his tyrannical regime. The militiamen then began fighting among themselves for power and control over the land and the government. During this bloody struggle, rival factions staked out their own areas to rule.

One of the hardest hit regions was the Jubba Valley, where an ethnic group known as the Bantus had quietly farmed for decades. The Bantus are descendants of people from the Southeast African countries of Tanzania and Mozambique who, during the nineteenth century, were captured by Arabs and sold into slavery in Somalia. Because they are ethnically, physically, and culturally different from Somalis, the Bantus have been victims of discrimination and prejudice even though slavery was abolished more than a century ago.

During the civil war, militias targeted the Somali Bantu farming villages, stealing livestock and crops and kidnapping people for ransom. Because the peace-loving Bantus had few weapons and no warlords to protect them, they were powerless to stop the militias. To escape war and famine, tens of thousands of Bantus trekked on *foot for weeks to neighboring Kenya, hoping life would be safer there in refugee camps.*

However, the Bantus still experienced hostility and inequality, so many moved to larger refugee camps farther from the Somali border. Unable to return to Somalia and rejected by those controlling their ancestral homelands, the Bantus were classified as a persecuted group and given priority refugee status by the United States. Between 2002 and 2007, more than 13,000 Bantus were resettled in America.

Although the worst of the civil war lasted through the 1990s, Somalia still is a country torn by ongoing conflict that, over the years, has claimed the lives of hundreds of thousands of innocent people.

Eleven-year-old Yussuf Yussuf watched an increasing number of strangers trudging on foot and pedaling on bicycles through his village in the Jubba Valley of Somalia. Many were lugging whatever possessions and provisions fit on their backs and heads. Some asked for food and water, which villagers readily offered.

The boy didn't know why so many were streaming past him. Soon he began hearing them say they were fleeing from war and violent militias, and that they were heading for the safety of a country called Kenya. He had never heard of such a place and had no idea where it was.

These refugees talked about how dangerous life in Somalia had become. *Danger?* He thought. *There's no danger here. I've never seen any signs of trouble.* Having no understanding that civil war was raging throughout the country, his fellow villagers laughed at the strangers for being such alarmists.

"Go ahead and laugh," Yussuf heard one passerby say. "But just you wait. One day soon, you will be the next to cry."

─────────────────

Yussuf lived the simple Bantu life in a family of subsistence farmers in southern Somalia. His village of about 200 people, Marerey, was considered relatively well off because everyone was self-sufficient and not dependent on anyone else, including the bigoted government, which despised the Bantus.

The boy and his four brothers and one sister tended to banana and mango trees as well as goats, chickens, and cows on the family farm with their father, Idris Yussuf Aden, and mother, Fatuma Mohamed Isaack. They lived in a large mud home with a grass roof right outside the village. Fatuma cooked over an open fire. The inside of the house had two rooms—a living room that had no tables or chairs and a bedroom. Their only furniture was a single bed that Idris had made for himself and Fatuma. The kids slept on mats on the dirt floor.

During the morning, Yussuf walked to Islamic school to learn the Koran and then attended regular school in the early afternoon. Although he was a bright student, he wasn't taught much about the rest of the world. His knowledge of life was confined to however far he could walk in his bare feet.

Possessing only a few pairs of shorts, T-shirts, and a ceremonial outfit, Yussuf never wore new clothes other than hand-me-downs. On weekends, he played soccer with kids from his village and went swimming in the nearby river. He assumed he would grow up and inherit some land and do exactly what his father and grandfather had done for decades—farm.

He had no concept of war or conflict because the Bantus were peace-loving people who wanted nothing more than to be left alone. Their only weapons were machetes, which they used to cut brush, and hoes, which they used to till the soil. The Bantus willingly shared their food and water with anyone—neighbor, stranger, or passerby—who was hungry or thirsty.

However, because of rampant prejudice and intolerance, the Bantus in Somalia were treated as second-class citizens by the government. Authorities would regularly show up at Bantu villages, examine the farmers' crops, and take half without paying for them. Even though Somali society marginalized the Bantus, Yussuf's father and the village elders didn't discriminate against anyone.

News traveled slowly to the region, and when it finally reached the Jubba Valley, the grown-ups didn't tell their offspring about the warring militias, partly because the Bantus thought the fighting would be confined to cities and towns. Early in 1992, Yussuf noticed that the one road through the village was becoming crowded every day with Somalians—mostly Bantus—who were making their way to Kenya.

One night, about 9:00 p.m., when families were falling asleep in their cozy mud huts, members of a fierce militia swooped into the village and immediately surrounded it so no one could escape. Brandishing their weapons, the rebels divided into groups and went door to door, demanding that the Bantu men step outside.

Two armed men, who covered their faces with bandannas, approached Yussuf's home and shouted to the startled family, "We know you're in there! Come out now!"

Idris emerged from the hut. As the rest of the family started to follow him out, the rebels ordered, "No! The rest of you stay inside."

Yussuf and the others listened in fearful silence as the rebels gruffly asked Idris a series of questions: "What kind of livestock do you own? How many cows? Where are they?"

When Idris was slow to respond, one rebel snapped, "Tell us everything, or we will kill your children!"

Yussuf had never felt terror until this night. *Are they going to shoot us?* he feared. His fright only grew worse when he heard from nearby huts children crying, rebels yelling, and adults protesting.

After Idris answered the rebels' questions, they ordered, "You come with us."

He didn't object. Before leaving with the gunmen, he told his family, "Stay calm and I will return."

Yussuf thought, *I'm not going to see Dad again.*

After gathering all the men in the village, the rebels held them at gunpoint in a field. "We need your animals, your crops, and your possessions," the rebels said. "If you don't give them to us, you die." There was no way for any of the Bantus to fight back because they were unarmed and outnumbered. Having displayed their might, the militia allowed the men to return to their homes.

The rebels brought Idris back to his hut and told him, "Take everything out of the house. If you don't, we will kill you and your children."

Yussuf was relieved to see his father again, but the boy was still terrified. *I don't think I'm going to make it out of here alive,* he told himself.

The gunmen rifled through the few possessions owned by the family and selected almost everything to take. This same scene of looting played out in every home in the village. The rebels forced Idris and the others to load the items onto the militia's pickups. Anyone who begged to keep something was threatened with death—a warning emphasized with gunshots fired into the air.

Yussuf watched helplessly as the rebels led away the family's 19 cows and 50 goats and grabbed all the chickens, too. When the militia took off later that night, Yussuf's family had nothing left but their clothes and a few empty water containers. *They didn't leave us with much of anything,* Yussuf thought. *They didn't leave anyone with much of anything. Our crops aren't ready to be harvested yet so we don't have much food. How are we going to survive?*

The next morning, the town crier called all the people to an emergency meeting at the big tree in the center of the village, where they had always held important gatherings. On the way there, Idris told his family, "I think it's time for us to leave because it's not safe here anymore. First, we will sit down and listen to the elders, who will figure out what all of us should do next. Whatever they say to do, that's what we will do."

At the meeting, the elders said they feared the militiamen would come back and do more harm. "If the rebels think we went to the police to report the looting—even though we didn't—they will return and kill everybody," said one of the elders. "We have come to one conclusion, and that is we must leave our beloved village for Kenya. It will be a hard and dangerous journey to the border. But there is no other way.

"To those of you who are ill or pregnant or too old to make it to Kenya, you can't stay here by yourselves. We will help you get to the next village, where you can remain for the time being until it is safe to return home—if it will ever be safe again."

Yussuf and his family gathered their remaining possessions and began the long 210-mile (338-kilometer) trek toward Dadaab, Kenya, site of a complex of refugee camps. Along the way, they were joined by an ever-growing flow of Bantus who were fleeing their villages, too. By the end of the first week, the number of refugees had reached more than 500.

It was the dry season, so there were few clouds to moderate

the high temperatures. The refugees typically walked early in the morning and then stopped and hid in the woods when the intense heat reached its peak of the day. "When the sun is on top of your head, it is not a good time to walk," Idris told Yussuf. "As your shadow moves away from you, that's when we walk again."

Their worst fear was encountering the rebels, so the group stayed off the main road and used paths in the forests whenever possible. The refugees tried to keep quiet because they didn't want to attract attention. Yussuf's youngest brother was only a year old, so his mother carried him the whole time to keep him from crying.

At night, the women and children slept under the stars or under the trees. The men, however, took shifts guarding the others. The only weapons the men had were heavy sticks, which weren't much protection against any lions, cheetahs, and rebels that lurked nearby. But it was all the Bantus had.

One day, Yussuf overheard two refugees talking about the rebels. "I don't think they will attack us," said one. "If they wanted to find us, they would have by now."

"I agree," said the other refugee. "I don't think they're looking for us because they figure we will die from hunger or thirst or exhaustion. They don't want to waste their time or effort on us."

During their afternoon breaks, Yussuf and his siblings often introduced themselves to young refugees from other villages. The kids didn't play with their new acquaintances because they didn't want to make noise. Besides, these breaks were the best time for Yussuf and his family to search in the woods for berries, mangoes, bananas, and wild sugar cane—anything that could ease the constant hunger gnawing in their bellies. The family ate just enough to survive, saving food to eat later or to share with those who were close to dying from starvation.

However, the biggest problem the refugees faced was thirst. For days, they trudged in the sweltering heat, barely with enough water to wet their parched throats. Yussuf and his family carried small 5-liter (1.3-gallon) bottles of water with them, which they rationed because they never knew from day to day where they would find water.

During their slow march across the stifling hinterlands of southern Somalia, they were constantly meeting people who had run out of water and were begging for a little sip from passersby. Yussuf's family offered their water whenever possible.

But one day, when the family was almost out of water, they encountered an elderly man sprawled on the road, his arm outstretched, pleading for a sip. Yussuf looked at his father to see if he would help the man. Idris sadly shook his head and kept on walking. "We don't even have enough water for ourselves," Idris told the boy. "If we give him the last of our water, then we'll all die from thirst."

People dying on the road—the old, the sick, the young—became a more common sight as the journey entered its second week. Seeing death up close left Yussuf feeling sad and helpless. He also wondered, *Could that be me soon?* Everyone was getting desperate for water.

Eventually, they came upon a small village that had a watering hole for humans to use for drinking. The mood of the distressed, thirsty refugees lightened—until they discovered grim-faced rebels were guarding the water and demanding fees from the travelers. No one could drink from it until the rebels were paid.

Two of Yussuf's friends were too dehydrated to think clearly. When the parched boys saw the water, they couldn't stand still and ran past the rebels. The angry gunmen fired their weapons in the air to stop them, but the kids kept going. By accident or on purpose, one of the rebels lowered his gun and fired several more rounds. As Yussuf and his fellow refugees looked on in shock, bullets struck and killed the two boys.

When the tragic reality of what just happened sunk in and people began wailing in anguish, Yussuf thought, *Am I next in line to be shot? Is my sister? My brothers? We're dying of thirst.* They were willing to do anything—even risk being shot—for the chance to drink.

After the cries of grief and outrage subsided, the rebels finally allowed the refugees to collect water in buckets, jugs, and other containers and pass them back to the others. The water quenched Yussuf's horrible thirst, but it left a bitter taste in his mouth because this water had led to the senseless killing of his two pals.

The journey continued. Day after day, the refugees walked until they were exhausted. Because Yussuf was small, skinny, and barefoot, there were a few times when he just couldn't keep up with the others. "Go on ahead," he told his parents more than once. "I'm going to rest and then catch up with you later." Because there was a steady procession of people, he was never alone. After a brief rest, he would hustle to reach his family.

Idris and Fatuma were always offering encouragement to Yussuf and his siblings. "Yes, it's difficult, but keep going," Idris urged his kids. "Things will improve once we reach Kenya and can make a better life for ourselves."

Fatuma kept reminding them that they were stronger as a family, and it was important to stick together. "I don't want to lose any of you, my children," she told them. "We have to look out for each other."

Yussuf believed his parents' words and pictured a happier life in Kenya. He was fueled by visions of eating all the food he wanted, drinking as much water as he could, and gobbling all sorts of yummy candies when they reached their new home. At times when he wanted to quit walking because he was too tired, hungry, or thirsty, he would murmur to himself, "Keep going, keep going, keep going."

They walked from one village to another, never stopping for more than a night. Some villagers were kind and offered food while others were too poor to share. Like almost all the refugees, Yussuf was getting weaker by the day.

In their third week of the journey, Yussuf and his family

were part of a group far ahead of other refugees as they entered a Bantu village near the Kenyan border. The villagers welcomed the fatigued, starving travelers and butchered a camel for them to eat. Many refugees were so malnourished that they suffered a bad reaction from eating solid food and became seriously ill. For the first few days, Idris and Fatuma gave their children only tiny portions of porridge and plenty of water to consume until they were well enough to eat solid food.

Because rebels were in the area, the refugees remained in the village for nearly a week until it was safe enough to continue. During their stay, the villagers continued to care for their fellow Bantus. Yussuf was even given his first pair of shoes ever—used flip-flops.

When the refugees finally reached the United Nations processing center at the Kenyan border, everyone cheered and hugged each other. They had made it despite the rebels, the heat, the hunger, the thirst, and the exhaustion.

Yussuf was happy and relieved. But the flow of refugees overwhelmed United Nations officials, causing the center to turn into chaos. Workers were herding refugees into trucks, which were heading to various refugee camps in the general area.

In all the confusion, Yussuf hopped onto a truck that he thought his parents and siblings were boarding. But when it took off without them, he realized he had jumped onto the wrong vehicle. It transported him to a bustling refugee camp near the Kenyan village of Dagahaley, where he waited for his family to arrive.

When they didn't show, Yussuf began to worry. He told officials he was separated from his family, but they brushed him off. In frustration and fear, he broke down and wept.

Fortunately, refugee Rashid Mohamed and his family, who came from Yussuf's village, spotted the crying boy and went over to help him. "Don't worry," said Rashid. "We will be here for you. You will stay with us while we help find your parents and hand you back to them."

He lived with the Mohamed family in a tent for what he thought would be for a few days. The camp had a billboard that listed the names of lost or separated refugee families, but he never saw his family's name on it. He studied the faces of arriving refugees who came through the camp gate, hoping he would recognize someone from his village who might have seen his family. He went up to Bantu refugees, told them he was from the Majindo tribe, and asked them if they ever heard of his father Idris or mother Fatuma. The answer was always the same: no.

Resigned that he might never see his family again, Yussuf accepted the Mohameds as his new family because they treated him as if he were their own flesh and blood. With the ongoing civil war in Somalia showing no signs of letting up, the Mohameds realized Dagahaley might be their permanent home, so they moved out of their tent and into a mud house they had built.

Yussuf went to school in camp where he learned basic English and improved on his Swahili and Somali language skills. He knew his parents were strong believers in education even though they never had the opportunity to attend school when they were his age. He read books and studied hard.

The years went by without any news of the whereabouts of his biological family. Yussuf continued to show up regularly at the United Nations office in the camp, hoping to find their names on a refugee list. When he was almost 18 years old, he decided to take matters into his own hands. "I am old enough to take care of myself," he told the Mohameds. "I'm returning to Somalia to try to look for my family."

Despite the violence, he made it safely back to his village only to learn his parents had not returned. However, he did find his uncle Talaso, who gave him wonderful news: Yussuf's family was alive and living in a refugee camp in Hagadera, which was only 10 miles (16 kilometers) away from the camp in Dagahaley.

Days later, Talaso escorted Yussuf to Hagadera, where, after an agonizing six-year separation, the teenager returned to his family in an emotional reunion. After all the crying and hugging, Yussuf asked his father, "Why didn't you look for me?"

"We tried many times," Idris replied. "We contacted the United Nations and checked the list of lost relatives on the billboard, but your name never showed up. I didn't have enough money to travel to the other refugee camps to look for you. We kept hoping the officials would find you for us. But now we are together again as a family."

Yussuf hesitated and said, "I know you are my parents, but the Mohameds raised me over the past six years as their son, and I want to stay with them."

"No, we cannot allow that," Idris said. "You are, and always will be, my son and a member of our family."

Yussuf understood, but he had become attached to the Mohameds. Then he came up with a suggestion: He would stay with his biological family if the Mohameds would move to Hagadera so that he could remain a part of both families. Everyone agreed to his solution.

The camp, which held tens of thousands of refugees, was not an ideal place to live because it was located in some of Kenya's most inhospitable terrain, where vast stretches of land were so arid that people celebrated whenever it rained. For the Bantus, who were used to farming, it was impossible to grow crops or find work. They were given meager rations and were subject to the same bigotry and discrimination they experienced in Somalia. Complicating their lives further, border-crossing Somali militiamen and local bandits periodically attacked them.

In 1998, when Yussuf was 18, he examined his future and didn't like what he saw. There was no way he could return to violence-torn Somalia. Kenya offered a few slightly better options, but only if he could get work in one of the big cities.

Because he could speak three languages, including English, he found work as a translator and an outreach worker for the

United Nations. He earned 3,500 shillings, or about 40 dollars a month, which was considered good money at the time. He gave all but 500 shillings (less than six dollars) to his father to help support the family.

In 2001, Yussuf became engaged to Muslimo Rasulow, a Bantu refugee he had known since childhood. That same year, the United States announced that Bantus were eligible for possible resettlement in the United States. To Yussuf, the United States was like another world—one that he imagined was populated by only white people (whom many Bantus called "Marble Eyes" because Americans had so many different eye colors).

Yussuf and Muslimo discussed with each other whether they wanted to alter their lives forever by going to America. The more Yussuf learned about the United States, the more excited he became. "I think America will give us a good life, and that I will be able to support our future family and send money back to my family here in Kenya," he told Muslimo. She agreed that they should take advantage of this monumental opportunity.

"It is still a scary decision," Yussuf told her. "We will be leaving everything behind that we know—the land, our neighbors, our friends, our culture, and our families. But it is right for us."

When Yussuf told his parents of the decision, Idris said, "If you want to go, please go. We give you our blessings." Idris, Fatuma, and Yussuf's siblings chose to stay in Kenya.

In 2002, the United Nations sent Yussuf and Muslimo more than 700 miles (1,126 kilometers) away to a refugee camp in Kakuma, Kenya, where the couple married two years later.

After both went through an extensive vetting process, including background checks, interviews, and physical examinations, authorities approved the couple for admission to the United States. On Yussuf's final interview, an immigration official told him, "Congratulations. You will be starting a new life in America." The official held out his hand. Yussuf grasped it and thought, *It's the first time I've ever shaken hands with a white man. It won't be my last.*

Yussuf and Muslimo, along with Yussuf's uncle Talaso and his family, arrived in Charlottesville, Virginia, in 2004. The International Rescue Committee (IRC) helped set the refugees up with places to live and arranged for other immediate needs until they could support themselves.

Within a month, Yussuf landed a job as a housekeeper, soon obtained a driver's license, and then earned his GED (General Education Development, the equivalent of a high school diploma). While working part time for the IRC as a translator, he found full-time employment as a maintenance man at Monticello, the famed plantation home of President Thomas Jefferson.

In 2012, Yussuf and Muslimo stood on the platform at Monticello's annual July Fourth ceremony and took the oath to become United States citizens. They live in Charlottesville, where they are raising their five sons, Abdikhayr, Isaack, Mohamed, Ismail, and Noordin.

"I feel it's all a miracle to me," Yussuf says. "I was working on the family farm in southern Somalia and years later here I am in America with my wife and five boys and a good job and a wonderful life."

THE HEART OF A REFUGEE

HEVAL MOHAMED KELLI
Syria

The Kurds are the largest ethnic group in the world without a homeland. Most of the more than 30 million Kurds live in Iraq, Syria, Iran, and Turkey.

In Syria, where they account for about 10 percent of the population, Kurds have been treated as second-class citizens for generations, facing routine discrimination and harassment by the government. Among the rights stripped from them: Kurds haven't been allowed to officially use the Kurdish language, register their children with Kurdish names, start businesses with names other than Arabic, build Kurdish private schools, nor publish books and other materials written in Kurdish. Thousands of Syrian Kurds have been denied citizenship, and their descendants have been labeled as foreigners.

Syria has a long history of human rights abuses of its citizens— no matter their ethnicity or religion—dating back to 1963, when the country was put under emergency rule that limited the rights of free expression and association and banned public gatherings of *more than five people. For more than half a century, powerful secret police and other security forces have arrested, detained, and tortured people—many of them innocent—who have been accused of being critics or enemies of the government.*

Civil war erupted in the spring of 2011 after security forces opened fire on protestors who had marched on the capital city of Damascus, demanding democratic reforms and the release of political prisoners. The conflict spread throughout the country between the Syrian army and a coalition of rebels with vastly different agendas among themselves. The hostilities have led to a growing death toll from heavy shelling, air strikes, and even chemical-weapons attacks on cities and towns. Depending on international estimates, between 200,000 and 470,000 people have died in a civil war that has continued to rage well into 2017. Nearly half the population of Syria—about 11 million people—have fled their homes, with nearly 4 million of them living as refugees in other countries.

Ten-year-old Heval Mohamed Kelli sensed from the violent pounding on the door of his home in Aleppo, Syria, that trouble stood on the other side.

When his stay-at-home mother, Saadia, opened the door, four scowling men—two in regular clothes and two in dark army-green uniforms wielding AK47s—barged in and began yelling at her. Several more uniformed men stood outside. Heval didn't know who they were or what they wanted. He had never encountered anyone like them before, and he was scared. So was his six-year-old brother, Mohamed, who scurried under his bed and hid from the intruders.

Too flustered to understand what the men were shouting, Heval watched in horror as they slammed Saadia brutishly against the wall. She fell hard to the floor, gashing open her leg against a glass table.

Instinctively, Heval scurried toward his mother to help her. But before the boy reached her, one of the soldiers struck him in the head with the butt of the AK47. Heval toppled to the floor in a daze. When he sat up, he felt blood running down his face and heard his mother crying out in protest.

"Why are you hurting me, and why are you hurting my child?" Saadia screamed at them.

"Shut up!" one of the men snapped.

"Why are you doing this?" she continued. "What do you want from us?"

"I said shut up!"

While the woozy boy held his bloody head and shook with fear, the men ransacked the well-appointed home, storming from one room to another, overturning furniture, flinging cushions, knocking over lamps, breaking artwork, and tossing framed photos onto the floor. They yanked out dresser drawers and overturned the contents and stripped clothes off hangers in the closets.

Heval remained on the floor, too frightened to move while the intruders continued their reckless rampage, displaying total disregard for the family's possessions. He didn't look at the men. All he could hear were the thumps of their boots on the ceramic floor and the crashing of glass and other breakable objects.

After five terrifying minutes, the men stomped out. If they were looking for something specific, they didn't find it. If they were trying to wreck the place, they succeeded. Saadia always took pride in keeping an immaculate home, which was now anything but that.

Ignoring the pain from her wounded leg, she checked on Heval's condition and then found Mohamed, who was still cowering under the bed. He was safe and unharmed.

As bad as the invasion was, the news that followed was even worse. Saadia tried to phone her husband, Kemal, who was a well-connected successful attorney, but she couldn't reach him. She soon learned that members of Syria's secret police—like the ones who had burst into her home—had abducted Kemal from his office and whisked him off to an unknown place.

When Heval heard that his father had been taken away, the boy thought, *I might never see Dad again. What's going to happen to my family? Are those men going to come back?* The fear he felt for his father, himself, and his loved ones overwhelmed Heval.

Members of Kemal's well-known and respected family rushed over to the home to comfort Saadia, Heval, and Mohamed. Heval was grateful for the support although he trembled when he overheard an uncle say, "If they come into your house, you know you are in big trouble."

Traumatized by his father's disappearance, Heval suffered

a seizure. It was as if his brain had short-circuited, causing him to lose all sense of awareness. When he came out of it a few minutes later, he had no recollection of the seizure. But he knew where he was and that bad men had ravaged his home. The upended furniture, the mess on the floor, and the dirty footprints on the carpeted area were reminders of what had just occurred, not that he needed any.

Over the next few days, the family pieced together what had happened to Kemal. The Syrian government, which always viewed the Kurdish people as a threat, knew Kemal had done legal work for his fellow Kurds. The secret police asked him to spy on his own people for the government. He declined. The authorities ramped up the pressure on him to comply when they made it clear their request to spy was now a demand. He still refused. That's when the secret police snatched him from his office and later stormed into his house.

"The secret police are to be feared because they don't follow the law," an uncle told Heval. "They can do whatever they want. Never look them in the eye and don't ever argue with them because they are like a feared monster. There is nothing and no one that can protect you from the secret police."

Until that fateful day, Heval never knew that his father could be in any danger in Syria. Kemal and Saadia had hidden the truth from their children about the government's oppression of the Kurdish people. Because of Kemal's legal skills and his relatively good relationships with authorities, he was able to provide his family with a stable, upper middle class life. They lived in a beautiful home in a desirable neighborhood in Aleppo and always were dressed in fashionable clothes. In fact, Kemal seldom left home without wearing a suit and tie. The family often dined in nice restaurants and went to the movies. To Heval, who attended a private school where he was an honor student, life in Syria was just fine.

The boy wasn't aware the government discriminated against the Kurds and had denied hundreds of thousands of them Syrian citizenship. He didn't know Kemal used his legal expertise and connections to secure citizenship for the entire family. Moreover, the boy had no clue his very name presented a problem because of bigotry. When Heval was born in 1983, Kemal tried to register his son's name, which means "friend" in Kurdish. But an official refused to authorize it because the government had banned all Kurdish names. However, being the influential attorney that he was, Kemal managed to win government approval of the name.

Several months after Kemal's disappearance, an influential family friend who had connections with Syrian officials helped free Kemal from a special prison that the secret police used to harbor political enemies.

When Kemal returned home, his appearance shocked Heval. The man who had been neatly groomed and well dressed in suit and tie now looked distressed and disheveled with unkempt hair and a face covered in thick stubble. His clothes were wrinkled and dirty. *He's not the same person I knew when I last saw him*, Heval thought.

After their tearful reunion, Kemal expressed concern for Heval's head injury and the gash on Saadia's leg. Her wound had become infected, causing her to require hospitalization to clear it up. Although Kemal tried to comfort everyone, he refused to talk to his sons about his arrest and confinement, believing the less they knew, the better.

He certainly didn't want to worry them by revealing the truth—that the secret police warned him, "The next time you get arrested, you might not come out of prison alive."

All Kemal told the boys was that the family was going to the neighboring country of Turkey for a while. They had to leave everything behind other than their clothes and a few personal possessions. Heval, who loved to draw and read mysteries, brought along colored pencils and several books. The family then sneaked out of Syria and drove to Turkey, where they stayed with friends of Kemal.

Having been uprooted from the only home he knew and not understanding exactly why his father was being persecuted, Heval tried to convince himself the move was temporary. *This is just one long bad nightmare that will end soon*, he thought. *We will all go back home, and everything will return to normal.*

However, shortly after arriving in Turkey, Kemal learned the secret police had arrested one of his brothers for helping him and his family escape from Syria. Upset by this terrible development, Kemal no longer withheld the truth from his sons, telling them, "We won't be going back home."

"Ever?" Heval asked in disbelief. His father nodded.

Kemal and Saadia tried to brush off Heval's concerns and worries, promising him that they all faced a much better future, although not necessarily in Turkey, a country that also discriminated against the Kurds.

About six weeks after their arrival in Turkey, Kemal announced to the boys, "We're going on a plane." He declined to tell them the destination or that a smuggler had obtained the necessary documents to get them out of the country. On their way to the airport, Kemal told the boys, "If anybody asks you where you are going, just tell them you are going on vacation. That's all you need to know."

With Heval's head still spinning from the abrupt departure, the family flew to Frankfurt, Germany, where they were transported to a refugee housing complex called a *Heimat* (a German word meaning "home"). A tall fence surrounded a big brown building that reminded Heval of a high school, only with guards at the door checking who came and went. Hundreds of refugees from various war-torn countries were housed here.

Heval and his family were not accustomed to the Spartan living conditions. They had to cope in a small room with two bunk beds, share a bathroom with everyone else on their floor, and wait in line for their cafeteria food. For an upper middle class family that had lived in comfort in Syria, this was a difficult adjustment, especially for Saadia.

The family eventually met other Syrian and Kurdish refugees and soon became friends. Even though kids of other nationalities spoke different languages, they communicated through gestures and smiles and were linked by common interests such as soccer and foosball (table soccer). After dinner, people gathered in the main hall and played their native music, sang, and danced in an international songfest. For a few captivating hours, the people could forget that they were refugees without a permanent home.

Heval didn't know what Germany was like outside the fence because few people were allowed to leave the *Heimat*. In fact, the only person in the family who got out was Kemal, and that was only for one brief time. After living there for six months, however, the family was shipped off to another *Heimat*, this one in the small town of Herscheid, in western Germany. The family moved into a two-room apartment and shared a bathroom with the next-door residents.

At least the refugees here were allowed to walk freely in the community, although that freedom came with a price— prejudice. Many Germans in town scorned the refugees, especially Muslims. When refugees went grocery shopping, they were easily identified because they paid with big red government-issued certificates. For proud Muslims like Heval and his family, who believed in hard work and self-reliance, this was degrading.

Heval attended school for the first time since fleeing Syria only to feel the sting of bigotry. On his first day, he donned a nice shirt and dress slacks, which were what he typically wore in Syria. But in Herscheid, students sported T-shirts and jeans.

Everyone avoided talking to the new nerdy, bespectacled kid who was still struggling with the German language.

A few days later, a glowering German student in military boots strode toward Heval and, without saying a word, gave him a violent shove. After backpedaling to maintain his balance, Heval charged forward and pushed his attacker. The German then socked Heval in the nose, knocking him to the floor.

Dazed from the blow, Heval sat up and touched his nose, which was bleeding badly. Some onlookers stared at him and others sneered. No one offered to help him. As the German walked away, the clomping of his boots and the blood dripping from Heval's face triggered the awful memory of the raid by the Syrian secret police. Heval was immediately shrouded in the same helplessness and anger that he had felt on that fateful day in Aleppo.

The unprovoked attack in school sent a signal to other students that it was all right to bully Heval and push him around. Each time he was victimized, a feeling of revenge swirled inside him. So did his rage.

One day at the end of the week, Heval walked out of school and spotted six rough-looking students who were similar to him in appearance—black hair and light brown skin. They approached him and started talking to him in Arabic. During the conversation, he learned they were refugees, too, from Iraq, Turkey, Albania, Bosnia, and Nigeria. They were known as the *Auslanders*, the German word for "foreigners."

As they chatted, the German student who had assaulted

him days earlier exited the building. "Do you see that guy over there?" Heval said to his new friends. "My first day in school, he punched me in the nose for no good reason. He and his pals have been harassing me ever since."

Mahmoud*, a student refugee who had a scar across his face, said, "Let me handle this." Glaring at the German, Mahmoud marched over to him. Heval noticed the German suddenly looked afraid and nervous—the same feelings that Heval had experienced right before the student had struck him days earlier. Unexpectedly, Mahmoud began slapping the German, who was much bigger than he was. Heval thought, *Oh, no, my new friend is going to get punched in the face.* But the German student stood there and took the licking. When the German's buddies didn't come to his aid, Heval grinned. *He and his friends know if they make a move to fight back, the* Auslanders *will jump them.*

At first, Heval savored the vengeance. He was happy to see the German get a taste of his own medicine. But when the slapping ended, Heval noticed the German's sad expression. In that face, Heval saw himself, remembering how he had felt when he was slugged. Revenge didn't feel nearly as good as he thought it would.

Heval became close friends with his fellow refugee ruffians, who had a reputation for being tough guys willing to fight anytime, anywhere. Once the German students saw that Heval was part of this gang, they didn't bother him again.

Feeling empowered and protected, Heval changed. He was

no longer the serious, obedient student; the thoughtful, polite teenager; the happy, helpful classmate. All the pent-up fury and frustration from losing his comfortable life in Syria, all the resentment and bitterness he held inside over being a stateless refugee had molded him into a virtual three-headed monster—a bully, a jerk, and a punk.

Heval didn't recognize himself anymore and didn't care. Fueled by all those negative emotions, he began harassing those who had once hassled him. He initiated several fights that often grew wilder when his friends jumped in, and he joined skirmishes that his pals started. Now a rebellious student, Heval stopped doing homework and began talking back to his teachers, even cursing one of them with German swear words taught to him by the gang. In Syria, he never would have behaved this way.

Repeatedly, school officials reprimanded him, gave him detentions, and made him stay after school to do extra work. The punishments didn't faze him because anger had consumed him. He was angry over leaving Syria and not being able to return. Angry over being poor and having no family income. Angry over not fully grasping the German language but fully understanding German prejudice. Angry over living in meager quarters and sharing a bathroom with neighbors. And angry over being welcomed at school with a punch in the nose.

At home, however, he seemed okay. That's because he lied to his parents, telling them he was doing fine in his studies and enjoying school. They had no reason to doubt him, knowing he had always been a straight-A student in Syria. He chose to keep his true feelings to himself, so his parents weren't aware how much he was suffering emotionally.

But one of his teachers, Herr Klose, knew and decided to do something about it. Herr Klose arranged a meeting that included him and Heval, Heval's dad, Kemal, and an interpreter. Kemal was smiling at first but as the interpreter explained how badly Heval was doing in school, Kemal began to sweat and frown. "How could my son go from an honor student to such a troubled kid so quickly?" Kemal asked. "I am so ashamed of him."

After the truth of Heval's behavior surfaced, Herr Klose told Kemal, "Heval is not acting like the son you raised. His behavior turned bad quickly. But that means with a shift in attitude and some extra help, which I'm willing to give, he could just as quickly turn back into the great kid he used to be."

On the walk home, Kemal didn't say a single word to Heval. When Kemal explained to his wife, Saadia, about their son's behavior at school, she was too stunned to be angry. Kemal told Heval, "I am very sad because you are our best hope for a better future. We have no money, no home, no country. But the one thing available to you is an education."

That night Heval cried in the shower. *I'm ashamed of myself*, he thought. *I've let my family down and I've let myself down.*

The next morning, Heval went to Herr Klose and said, "I want to become a better student and a better person. Will you help me?" Every day after that, Heval came to school early so

Herr Klose could spend time teaching him how to read, write, and speak German—and how to channel negative feelings into positive behavior.

Heval still hung out with his refugee friends. Seeing how serious he was about his studies, they became supportive and protective of him. They made sure he wasn't involved in any more fights and kept encouraging him to be the best student in school. "If any refugee can make it out of here with a future, it's you, Heval," said Mahmoud. They were proud of him and wanted to see him succeed. But one by one, the *Auslanders* dropped out of school. They were simply too tormented by the horrors they had experienced that had forced them to flee their homelands.

For Heval, all the studying paid off. He soared to the top of his class, and after tenth grade, was one of the school's few students bright enough to attend gymnasium—the highest level of schooling before college. For the first time since fleeing Syria, Heval had dreams he believed were achievable—going to college and then medical school and finally becoming a doctor.

However, there was a hitch. Every six months for the previous five years, his parents had applied for permanent residency, which the German government had failed to grant. Living as an asylee meant that Heval couldn't advance to college. The 16-year-old had lost hope. *I worked and studied so hard to become educated, and for what?* he fumed. *I can't go on to college. It's so frustrating. I might as well give up because what's the use of trying?*

Maybe I should be like my friends. No homework, just hang out at the youth center, get in trouble, and have fun. That's the easiest thing to do. I'll be like them in a year anyway. He was, after all, a refugee.

Periodically, a church lady in Herscheid would arrive at the *Heimat* in a truck filled with donated used clothes and kitchen items for refugees. At first, Heval and his parents were too proud to pick through the donations. But for a family too poor to go to the movies or a restaurant, they eventually accepted the help.

To Heval, sorting through the clothes was like a fun treasure hunt. But because his chances of a higher education had vanished, he was now depressed. So when he found a cool Nike jersey among the donations, he didn't show his usual excitement, which the church lady noticed and asked him why. Opening up to her about his frustrations, Heval said, "We have no country, no future, no hope," he complained. "Germany doesn't want us, and we have nowhere else to go."

"Why not apply for entry into Canada or the United States?" she suggested. "It's a long shot—a very small chance—but we'll help you and your family with the application. You have nothing to lose by trying."

Kemal had all the documents ready and, with the church lady's assistance, applied for refugee status to America. To Heval, the United States meant Levi's jeans, hip-hop music, and McDonald's Quarter Pounders. And freedom.

The process dragged on for more than a year. Then one

day, the church lady showed up at the *Heimat* with an official letter. It said the family had been approved for refugee status in the United States. Heval, his parents, and brother wept with joy. Then Heval uttered words he never dreamed he would ever say: "I'm going to be an American!"

With no friends or family in the United States, Heval, his brother, Mohamed, and their parents boarded a plane for America two weeks after the 9/11 terrorist attacks in 2001. On the plane, the family worried and wondered: How are they going to treat us when they see we are Muslims? Are they going to chase us down the street? Will we get harassed?

The family eventually arrived in Atlanta, where a Somalian refugee greeted them and drove them to their apartment in Clarkston, Georgia (population 7,700), a town with more resettled refugees per capita than anywhere else in the country. "Finally, I was at a place where we were wanted," Heval recalls today. "No longer was there fear of being shipped back or of secret police barging in."

All Saints' Episcopal Church in Atlanta furnished the family's apartment and stocked the cupboards. Every week for a year, a volunteer showed up to teach them English. Anonymous church members paid the family's rent for six months, helped them get a car, and paid Heval and Mohamed to cut their lawns and babysit their kids.

"The fact that an Episcopalian church would open its hearts,

wallets, time, and effort to help a Muslim family shows what a great country America is," Heval says. "These people didn't care what our religion was or where we come from. They truly wanted to help us. They saw something in us that we didn't see in ourselves."

While attending high school, Heval worked 30 hours a week at the Mediterranean Grill in Atlanta, washing dishes and cleaning bathrooms for five dollars an hour. "At the restaurant, I would see doctors in scrubs and I would tell myself, 'I want to be one of them one day,'" he recalls. "First, I needed to read and write English, so I made myself a promise that for every dish I washed, I would read one page of a book, magazine, or newspaper on weekends and nights. Three hundred plates, three hundred pages. I read lots of books about the Holocaust to help me with my English, which I learned in four months." He graduated with a 4.0 grade point average and earned a Hope scholarship that allowed him to enroll at Georgia State University (GSU).

His mother became an assistant day-care teacher at a Baptist church. Kemal was unable to work because he suffered from heart problems, depression, and PTSD (post-traumatic stress disorder) caused by his imprisonment and the war in Syria.

While attending GSU, Heval continued to work at the restaurant and took on other jobs to support the family. He remained focused on one day becoming a doctor. The kitchen counter that steamed up from the commercial dishwasher served as his whiteboard, which allowed him to trace, with his fingertip, molecular structures for organic chemistry. He read textbooks during breaks and talked to restaurant patrons who were students and doctors from nearby Emory School of Medicine.

Meanwhile, Barbara Thompson, who headed Solutions for Interrupted Education, a nonprofit organization that helps child survivors of war thrive in the classroom, took a special interest in Mohamed. With her help and that of the church, he received a scholarship to a private school, Pace Academy, where he excelled in soccer.

Then came a moment of serendipity. "Mohamed happened to tell a classmate that I was a sophomore at GSU and was washing dishes to help support the family, and that I wanted to become a doctor," Heval recalls. "Over dinner, this classmate happened to tell her father." The girl's father was Dr. Omar Lattouf, a respected cardiothoracic surgeon and Emory School of Medicine professor with family roots in Jordan, Palestine, and Lebanon. "He called me out of the blue," Heval says. "I was suspicious. Why would a well-known heart surgeon want to talk to a dishwasher who was a refugee?"

Dr. Lattouf invited Heval to his home and was impressed with the young man. Recalls Heval, "He asked me to help him with research. It was a test to see how motivated I was. He asked for one report, and I found ten and gave them to him. He became my mentor, invited me to research conferences, and introduced me to some of his colleagues. He motivated me and helped me apply to medical schools."

Heval graduated with honors in a premedical curriculum at GSU and enrolled in Morehouse School of Medicine in Atlanta. No longer washing dishes at the restaurant, he focused on his studies and graduated cum laude from medical school in 2012. He completed his residency in internal medicine at Emory School of Medicine—which was a few blocks from the Mediterranean Grill.

In 2015, Heval was named a Katz Fellow in Preventive Cardiology, a prestigious award that covered two years of generous salary, benefits, and expenses for research and related travel in anticipation of a career in academic cardiovascular prevention. He began publishing medical papers, traveling for academic presentations, and working on projects with the Georgia Department of Public Health and the Centers for Disease Control and Prevention, the nation's health protection agency.

With the money he earned as a doctor, Heval bought his parents a house in nearby Snellville, Georgia. Meanwhile, Mohamed attended Wofford College in South Carolina on a soccer scholarship and then followed his brother's example by going to medical school. In 2016, Mohamed was completing his residency in general surgery at East Tennessee State University.

Heval follows the Kurdish saying, "Whoever taught you the letters, you owe them a book." Committed to giving back to the community that helped him achieve his American dream, he volunteers at the Clarkston Community Health Clinic, which provides free medical care to the uninsured. The clinic is located one block from the apartment that he and his family lived in when they arrived as refugees.

He helped Dr. Lattouf and community leaders create a nonprofit organization, UBeyond, for mentoring young people from underserved backgrounds. Heval also cofounded several nonprofits that focus on medical and health education, including You4Education and You4Prevention. He started the Young Physician Initiative, a program in his former high school in Clarkston to inspire students, many of them refugees, to go into the medical field. "It's a way to recreate my story," says Heval.

"As a fellow at Emory in cardiology, I want to be a leader in finding more effective ways to prevent heart disease and to be a health advocate in underserved communities. I'm dedicated to improving the lives of people." He is developing a cell phone app that would help a person keep track of his or her medical information and would send reminders of nearby inexpensive or free medical assistance.

"One positive incident, one helping hand, can change your life. In my case, I had several helping hands," Heval says. "It's not all about hard work. All the opportunities that were available to me were because of people in the church, mentors, and the Katz Foundation. I am so grateful to them and remain in touch with everyone who helped me."

Adds Heval, who became an American citizen in 2006 along with the rest of his family, "Americans should see a refugee as an investment and not a burden. If you can invest in one person, that person can be something special. Many people invested in me, and because of that I became a cardiologist. It could only happen here in America."

AFTERWORD

No one chooses to be a refugee. The United Nations High Commissioner for Refugees (UNHCR) says that as of 2017, conflict has forcibly displaced more than 60 million people because of their race, religion, political opinion, national origin, or ethnicity. To put this in perspective, that number roughly equals the combined populations of North Carolina, Florida, Georgia, and New York.

This means that about 1 out of every 125 people worldwide has fled from his or her home, the highest share of the world's population that has ever been forcibly displaced since 1951, when the UNHCR began collecting data on this issue. About 1 out of every 20 people living in the Middle East is displaced.

To be clear, there is a difference between refugees and immigrants. Refugees have no choice but to leave their homes and flee from armed conflict or persecution to save their lives or to preserve their freedom. They usually find temporary sanctuary and protection (known as asylum) in refugee camps or communities in neighboring countries.

Immigrants, on the other hand, are people who *choose* to move to another country, not out of fear but to be closer to family or to improve their educational or economic opportunities. They seek to establish legal residency and eventual citizenship in their adopted country. (In the United States, an estimated 11 million immigrants are undocumented, which means they are living here without having gone through the legal process for admission.) Victims of economic hardship, earthquakes, famines, floods, and other kinds of natural disasters are not considered refugees because they can return to their homeland without fear of violence or persecution once the crisis is over.

Americans have welcomed refugees from all over the world. More than 3.3 million refugees have arrived in the US since 1975, according to the State Department's Refugee Processing Center. The countries of origin of refugees who resettled here have changed over time, reflecting the various crises that have flared up during the past four decades. The annual number of refugee arrivals in the United States peaked at about 210,000 in 1980 because of a large wave of refugees from Vietnam and Cambodia. In the 1990s, refugees tended to come here due to political turmoil in the former Soviet Union and the genocide that followed the breakup of Yugoslavia.

From October 1, 2015, to September 30, 2016, the largest numbers of refugees have come from the following countries: Democratic Republic of Congo (16,370), Syria (12,587), Burma (also known as Myanmar) (12,347), Iraq (9,880), and Somalia

(9,020). Nearly half of these refugees, 46 percent, were Muslim compared to 44 percent who were Christian.

If refugees can't return home because it's unsafe and, for various reasons, can't immigrate to a neighboring country, the UNHCR considers them possible candidates for resettlement to a third country such as the United States. They must undergo a comprehensive, lengthy screening process (known as vetting) that includes personal interviews, medical examinations, and thorough background security checks. This process often takes more than two years to complete.

After the refugees are approved for admission to the US, they are given a detailed orientation that teaches them about important aspects of American life and culture, helps them develop problem-solving skills, and provides them with realistic expectations about resettlement. They must find a sponsor or borrow money to pay for the cost of transportation.

Refugees have been resettled in small towns, big cities, suburban communities, and rural regions throughout our country. If they have relatives who already live in the United States, they likely will be resettled nearby. Otherwise, organizations that work with refugees will place them in selected areas based on the availability of jobs, housing, and social services. These agencies welcome refugees at the airport; arrange for their housing, furniture, and basic household supplies; conduct orientation; help arrange English as a second language classes; and refer them to social services and job opportunities. The federal government provides refugees with financial aid for their first 90 days. Then they are on their own. Many, though, still receive help through churches, sponsors, and nonprofit charitable organizations.

For most refugees who resettle in the United States, their struggles are far from over. Adjusting to life in America can be extremely difficult. The adults need to find steady jobs, secure long-term housing, learn English, understand public transportation, handle shopping, and adapt to an entirely new culture.

Kids face a strange new world, too. Imagine this: You are a child refugee arriving in the United States, which is a foreign country to you, and you don't speak English. You go to school and quickly discover how difficult it is to make friends, communicate with your teachers, and take the bus without getting lost. You've been put in a class based on your age rather than your ability to grasp English, so you struggle to keep up with the other students. You are teased and bullied because of the way you look, the way you dress, the way you speak. Your parents don't have the education or language skills to help you. How, you wonder, can you conquer all these challenges?

It's not easy, but most young refugees like those in this book ultimately succeed by working hard and taking advantage of the opportunities this country offers. They grow up to become productive members of society—and in many cases, naturalized citizens of the greatest nation on earth. Among today's celebrities who were child refugees: singer Gloria Estefan (Cuba), NBA star Luol Deng (South Sudan), rapper K'nann (Somalia), actress Mila Kunis (Ukraine), actor Andy Garcia

(Cuba), musician Wyclef Jean (Haiti), supermodel Alek Wek (South Sudan), and former secretaries of state Madeleine Albright (Czechoslovakia) and Henry Kissinger (Nazi Germany).

As businesswoman Adenah Bayoh says, "What makes America really America is that my story wouldn't happen anyplace else but here. I'm a woman, I'm a black, and I'm a refugee."

ABOUT THE AUTHOR

Allan Zullo is the author of more than 100 nonfiction books on subjects ranging from sports and the supernatural to history and animals.

He has introduced Scholastic readers to the 10 True Tales series, gripping stories of extraordinary persons who have met the challenges of dangerous, sometimes life-threatening, situations. Among the books in the series are *Young Civil Rights Heroes*; *Police Heroes*; *FBI Heroes*; *Heroes of 9/11*; *Heroes of Pearl Harbor*; *Vietnam War Heroes*; *World War I Heroes*; *World War II Heroes*; *War Heroes*; *Voices from Iraq*; and *Battle Heroes: Voices from Afghanistan*. In addition, he has authored five books about the real-life experiences of young people during the Holocaust— *Survivors: True Stories of Children in the Holocaust*; *Heroes of the Holocaust: True Stories of Rescues by Teens*; *Escape: Children of the Holocaust*; *We Fought Back: Teen Resisters of the Holocaust*; and *10 True Tales: Young Survivors of the Holocaust*.

Allan, the father of two grown daughters and the grandfather of five, lives with his wife, Kathryn, near Asheville, North Carolina. To learn more about the author and his books, visit his website at www.allanzullo.com.